SHADES OF MY FOREFATHERS

SOLOMON ETTING
By AUGUSTIN EDOUART
Courtesy of the late Mr. Erskine Hewitt, New York City

Shades of My Forefathers

BY

HANNAH R. LONDON

WITH A FOREWORD BY

JOHN HAYNES HOLMES

SPRINGFIELD, MASSACHUSETTS

THE POND-EKBERG COMPANY

1941

FOR ROBERT

CONTENTS

[VII]

LIST OF ILLUSTRATIONS

[IX]

FOREWORD

PORTRAITS *of Jews by Gilbert Stuart and other Early American Artists** was an unforgettable book. Miss London did a priceless service in assembling a superb collection of pictures, in showing through these pictures the conspicuous and impressive part played by Jews in the early years of the American republic, and in revealing the altogether extraordinary character and culture of these Jews. Happy the nation which has such men and women among its citizens!

In this second book Miss London repeats her original unique achievement. In addition to portrait paintings, she has now found great numbers of early American silhouettes, and among these, as among the paintings, many Jewish faces and figures. With abounding enthusiasm and untiring energy, she has gathered together some fifty of these silhouettes of Jews and published them in this handsome volume, together with accompanying chapters of comment and description which themselves have great artistic and historical value.

Shades of My Forefathers interests me enormously from at least two points of view:

First, there is the endless fascination of the silhouette as a form of portraiture. Its origins in the profile pictures of ancient times, its development into a definite technique in modern times, its wide-spread practice by a variety of artists in the first half of the nineteenth century, comprise a chapter in the history of art which is as absorbing as it is important. Such shadow portraits as those included in this volume reveal accomplishment of rare distinction. There is beauty as well as character depic-

*Published by William Edwin Rudge; New York, 1927.

tion in this work. One almost feels regret at the appearance of photography which brought suddenly to an end a most delicate and difficult form of art.

Secondly, there is the momentous record contained in this book of the place held by the Jews in the social, commercial and cultural life of early America. Here Miss London repeats and extends the impression conveyed by her volume of *Portraits*. Some of the Jews presented in these pages are the same as in the earlier book. But most of the men and women are new, and yet embody the same pre-eminent qualities of personal grace and intellectual and spiritual power. These are remarkable people — men of high standing and repute, women of exceptional beauty and refinement, citizens of indispensable value to a free and enlightened community. Miss London's first collection of pictures was hailed as "a most valuable contribution to the history of the Jews in the United States." This second gallery is a fresh contribution of similar value. The two books constitute together an unanswerable challenge to the ignorance and indecencies of anti-Semitism.

I count it a privilege to place on record, here, my sense of indebtedness to Miss London. To speak with her, and to pore over her pages, is to discover that she has found her work itself to be a rich reward. But to this must be added the immeasurable gratitude of all who would further the cause of truth, goodness and beauty in the world.

JOHN HAYNES HOLMES

PREFACE

AFTER the publication of my book, *Portraits of Jews by Gilbert Stuart and other Early American Artists,* my attention was directed to a number of silhouettes of American Jews listed in the *Catalogue of American Portraits by August Edouart.*

This *Catalogue* compiled by Mrs. E. Nevill Jackson, the well-known English authority on silhouette history, lists thirty-eight hundred profiles, signed and dated by the artist, who visited us here from 1839 to 1849.

The silhouettes listed were compiled from Mrs. Jackson's own collection of Edouart's American profiles, and most of them, I was informed could be seen at the home of Reverend Glenn Tilley Morse of West Newbury, Massachusetts, most renowned of the silhouette enthusiasts.

It was always delightful to spin over the road to West Newbury, taking the Turnpike, and cutting through at Dummer Academy over the quiet and winding back-roads, enchanted alike by hill-top views and picturesque New England cottages to visit Mr. Morse and chat with him about his hobby.

He treasures by far the most extensive American collection of profile portraits by foreign and native artists; every type and size are represented. Some of these were snipped with scissors; some were hollow-cut; others painted, drawn, engraved, or modeled.

Arresting the attention are striking portraits in original frames of mellowed maple, and group profiles mounted against lithographed or sepia-washed backgrounds. There are miniature silhouettes on rings and in brooches tucked away in

[3]

cabinets, and upstairs is the famous Edouart Collection of American profiles hanging on the walls or filed away in folios.

It was no easy task to single out the Edouart silhouettes of Jews. But with Mr. Morse's kind assistance a few were found at each visit. At length it seemed expedient to assemble them for this book with other silhouettes tracked down from various sources.

As my collection grew apace, I would often think of the late Mr. Frank W. Bayley, whom I assisted at the Copley Gallery, Boston. Here I was first enthralled by research in American art. He was interested in my work, as was also the late Lawrence Park, eminent antiquarian. I owe much to their kindness. I also wish to express my thanks to the following from whom I have received inspiration and encouragement in the publication of my work: the late Frederic F. Sherman, Mr. John D. Pond, my publisher; Reverend John Haynes Holmes, Mr. Lee M. Friedman, Mr. Roger W. Straus, Reverend Henry Wilder Foote, Mr. Paul M. Herzog, Mr. Mark M. Horblit, Mr. Frederick F. Greenman, Mr. Mark Bortman, and Judge Jacob J. Kaplan.

The silhouettes in the Massachusetts Historical Society, the Boston Athenæum, the Essex Institute, the Museum of the City of New York, and the American Antiquarian Society, were of great value to me, as background material to the subject. I am indebted to these Societies, as well as to the individuals from whom I have received letters and permission to copy their portraits, and to my husband, Benjamin M. Siegel, for reading the manuscript. Furthermore, I shall welcome corrections and additional information on my subject.

HANNAH R. LONDON

BROOKLINE, MASSACHUSETTS
June, 1941

I

THE PROFILE IN HISTORICAL PORTRAITURE

MANY accomplished profilists practised their art in America, during the colonial period to the advent of photography in 1859. These artists as well as others, have received engaging treatment in the beautifully illustrated and indispensable books on profile portraiture by Mrs. Ethel Stanwood Bolton and Mrs. Alice Van Leer Carrick of New England; by Mr. Desmond Coke and Mrs. E. Nevill Jackson of London.

I made constant reference to the valuable source material in their work, which not only enumerates the biographical history and technique of numerous craftsmen, but also reveals absorbing interest on the art in its entirety.

The delineation of the profile portrait as an art has come down to us since ancient times. Egyptian tombs with their mummy cases and frescoed walls abound in this type of portraiture. It is observed, too, in the classical vase painting of the Greeks and Etruscans; in the manuscript art of Mediæval Persia, and in the professional work of a guild of profilists of sixteenth century Constantinople.

In historical portraiture the shade revealed itself to France during the latter part of the eighteenth century when excavations in central Italy brought to light Etruscan vases ornamented with profile paintings. Patterned on motives of Greek origin, the black shadows depicted scenes in the daily life, the household arts, children happily playing at games, the hunt and warfare.

The French imitated these shades in various forms of artistry, and approached with tremendous enthusiasm the revival of classical art, prevalently expressed during this period.

The vogue for the shadow portrait received further encouragement from Madame de Pompadour, mistress of Louis XV, and from Étienne de Silhouette, financial minister, to whom in 1759 fell the task of relieving a dissolute and extravagant court from its financial difficulties.

Monsieur de Silhouette's methods, however, were scarcely approved. In satirical mood, the Parisians, soon aware of his petty methods of taxation, began to dub everything that connoted the cheap or the small — "silhouette." And the little black shade which could be bought for only a few francs came to be known by that name. The French finance minister, forced to resign, turned out some very good profile pictures when he turned to the art for a hobby.

But the word *Silhouette* was not popularly associated with the profile-picture until 1826, when Augustin Edouart, an émigré Frenchman, who had fled to England, advertised himself as "Silhouettist." Though Edouart gave the accepted name to the craft, other professionals applied the words *Skiagraphy* and *Shadowgraphy* to their art. Some profilists were known as *Scissorgraphists,* and Hubard called himself a "Papyrotomist."

Among the silhouettists of England to develop a remarkable skill, and an individual technique, were Mrs. Pyburg of London Town, who, in 1699, made profile portraits of William of Orange and Queene Mary, and a Mrs. Harrington, known to have practised her art in 1775. We read of Miers and Field of London, who painted profiles on chalk, of the celebrated Charles, of a Mrs. Beetham's exquisite work, and the popular Rosenberg of Bath. Outstanding in the field were also Hubard,

Hankes, and Edouart who cut accurate likenesses with amazing rapidity.

Interesting examples of their silhouettes were collected by the late Mr. Montague Guest and subsequently purchased by Mr. Francis Wellesley. Some of them illustrate his exquisite and notable book, *One Hundred Silhouette Portraits Selected from the Collection of Francis Wellesley.*

The fashion for the silhouette was not only a great success in England, where amateurs and professionals vied with one another to create and excel, but it was carried over into Russia whence Mr. Glenn Tilley Morse says he has seen the very finest examples. In Austria the silhouette was sponsored by the royal family who took to the art for pastime, and in Germany it was extensively used for book illustrating.

Here it was further popularized by John Caspar Lavater, clergyman of Zurich, who wrote *Essays on Physiognomy Calculated to Extend the Knowledge and the Love of Mankind.* This scientific tome is profusely illustrated by silhouette portraits to emphasize his theory that the features and contour of the head reveal an understanding of the human soul.

Many silhouettes were sent to Lavater in the expectation of an interesting character reading, or with the hope of sudden fame in the event that Lavater would favorably use the portrait in his publications.

Even Goethe practised the art, which fascinated him. And its popularity was enhanced by numerous exhibitions, held during the eighteenth century, at Berlin, Brünn, Danzig and Düsseldorf, when royalty, warriors, statesmen, artisans of every profession — the great and small — were featured in the shadow portrait.

The silhouette flourished also during the Georgian period, lending itself to many forms of artistic expression. Generally the profile was scissored, painted, or drawn, on plaster or paper. Exquisite reductions to miniature size, mounted in rings and pins, and set with jewels were often made for gifts. The profile was also modeled in wax, engraved on copper, or printed in books. It was practised in China painting and etched on glass. Many examples of this latter work, colored, in black, or in clear white, are found in the Victoria and Albert Museum.

In the Theatre, as well, the shadow portrait proclaimed itself. Old Egypt, China, India, and Java made use of the shadow-portrait in their silhouette theatre. Still enacted in Java are their legendary scenes handed down from generation to generation, of which Mr. Hubert Stowitts has captured the spirit in his paintings, recently exhibited at the Boston Museum of Fine Arts.

In Javanese traditional manner little puppets were carved and painted; their shadows were projected on a white screen, while the performers remained hidden and the various parts were spoken. The illusionary effects thus created are revealed in an eleventh century record, culled from Mrs. Anne Holliday Webb's accompanying article on the Stowitts exhibit. "There are some who looking at the figures on the stage, do weep, feel sad, and are bewildered, though they know them to be only cut leather that pretends to speak."

With its historic and artistic background, the profile portrait whether scissored, drawn, or painted, engraved or modeled remains a notable collector's item. Before the advent of photography in this country, in 1859, this form of portraiture was most customary. It was inexpensive and its novelty captured the fancy of the Americans.

Recently — but long after collecting the material for this book — at the request of Mr. Carl J. Wennerblad, State Director of the Massachusetts Historical Records Survey, I launched a *Federal Survey* of profile portraits.

Excluding the four thousand profile portraits in the Glenn Tilley Morse Collection, the *Federal Survey* lists about six thousand American profiles. Included are the portraits illustrated or mentioned in publications and collections. We noted all the silhouettes in the Essex Institute and the Peabody Museum, of Salem; the Todd Album from the Boston Athenæum; the Henry W. L. Dana Collection, with its Class Album of Bowdoin College, 1825; the Bostonian Society; the Wadsworth Athenæum and the Henry Erving Collection in Hartford.

In addition many Historical Societies and Universities throughout the country reported on their profile portraits, as did many individuals who treasure ancestral shades.

The late Mr. Frederic F. Sherman, author of a number of important publications on early American portraiture, sent me a list of the profile portraits in his possession together with collected notes on various profilists. Their names, unfamiliar to me, are Alexander H. Emmons, Galoway, G. Catlin, Silas Dewey, Mary B. Tucker, and Justin Salisbury.

The manuscript, *Workers with Line and Color in New England, 1620-1870,* by Mr. Charles K. Bolton which reposes in the Boston Athenæum, notes other unfamiliar names of profilists. William Stevenson, a silhouettist of Vermont, 1822, is mentioned here as well as a Mr. Elliot, and a James Guild of Vermont, who traveled widely, kept an amusing diary, and was a great wag.

The work of all these artists should be included in the *Survey,* if it is ever resumed. Then, too, there are many silhouettes to be noted in Bache's Scrapbook, owned by Mrs. C. R. Converse, of Elmira, New York, and those in the possession of Mrs. Maurice P. Spillane, of Quincy, and Mr. Mark A.

De Wolfe Howe, of Boston. The late Mrs. Robert Hale Bancroft owned a sizable collection, as did also the late Mr.
Erskine Hewitt, of New York. The silhouettes in the American Antiquarian Society, the New York Historical Society,
and the Metropolitan Art Museum, should also be listed.
Information on these silhouettes would make a notable contribution to the history of profile portraiture in this country.

The modeled portraits in wax are noted in the *Federal
Survey of Portraits for New York and New England,* under
the direction of Mr. Charles K. Bolton, the former librarian
of the Boston Athenæum.

When, for financial reasons, the *Silhouette Survey* was unfortunately terminated in December, 1936, Mr. Bolton wrote:

I have read the outline of your work with appreciation. Mr. Wennerblad and I both had faith in you. I too am sorry to have the work stop
at this point — yours and mine. It was work of permanent value. But
there is a call for economy in Washington and we were obvious targets.

Many silhouettists are represented in the *Federal Survey.*
The hollow-cut variety abounds in the work of William Bache,
William Chamberlain, Moses Chapman, William M. S. Doyle,
Everet Howard, F. P. Jones, William King, R. Letton, Charles
Willson Peale, George (?) Todd, and Henry Williams.

There are profiles in natural tints by Cottu, Michel Felix
Cornè, Augustus Day, Thomas Edwards, James Sanford Ells-
worth, Fevret de Saint-Mémin, Thomas Gimbrède, William
James Hubard, John Wesley Jarvis, Rembrandt Peale, Edwin
Plummer, Essex Ridley, Rossiter, and T. Nixon.

Also listed are the profiles painted in India ink by William
Bache, Samuel Folwell, Jean François Vallée, John Joye, and
others. A. B. Doolittle, C. P. Polk, and Joseph Wood engraved

on gold; they, too, are noted. Of course, many of the silhouettists displayed versatility in varying their technique.

Included in the *Survey* are profile drawings by Fevret de
Saint-Mémin taken with a physionotrace, as well as his reduced
engraved portraits.

Then there are the scissored profiles. They were taken full-
length by Augustin Edouart, William Henry Brown, William
James Hubard, Philip Lord and Samuel Metford. Cut and
pasted they were mounted on plain, lithographed, or water-
colored backgrounds. Hubard also expressed himself in the
scissored bust profile, as did Master Hankes.

Wafered in the pages of Mrs. Bolton's own copy of her book,
Wax Portraits and Silhouettes, are valuable notes on some
rather obscure silhouettists, which I noted in the *Survey.*
Among them, a hollow-cutter, John Thompson; Mr. J. H.
Gillespie, of London, who worked in Halifax; E. Metcalf, and
Samuel Moore. She also writes of Martin Griffing of Rich-
mond, Massachusetts. Crippled for life, at twenty-two, after
a fall from a church steeple, which he was painting, he became
a profilist. He worked in Berkshire and adjoining counties, in
Vermont and New York State. Where are his silhouettes?

If the *Survey* is eventually concluded it will provide much
useful information on the subject. The silhouette, like the
family Bible, often yields invaluable records. Very often a
profile portrait is inscribed with the name of the sitter and
artist; also dates, an occupation, and a place of residence, sup-
plied by the profilist or furnished by the sitter or some member
of his family.

The completed study would also reveal the identity of a
number of silhouettists, whose work is neither stamped nor
signed, by the method they employed. The bust line frequently
distinguishes some profilists; or a characteristic trick of subtly

touching up the silhouette; or the foot or background. A clue, in addition, is often discovered by the frame, as some of the artists made them from their own design. And, too, many striking examples, thought to be only in the large collections will, no doubt, come to light from hidden corners.

Accumulatively they are worth thousands of dollars. For today the silhouette ranges in price from five to one hundred dollars, and unusual portraits of important people command considerably more.

Charming in their original frames, many of which can be seen in the Essex Institute, or even in reproductions, they enhance the background, whenever artistically arranged of almost any decorative scheme.

A renaissance in the art of silhouette is seen now in the work of the Baroness Eveline von Meydell, Mr. David Vernon, and Mr. Ugo Mochi.

II

METHODS OF TAKING THE PROFILE
PORTRAIT

THE various and clever methods which were employed by the artists in taking the profile portrait are in themselves absorbingly interesting.

The scissored and the modeled profile; at times, the painted and the drawn, were taken from life without mechanical intervention. Very often, too, a piece of paper fastened to the wall, caught the sitter's profile which was traced. This was an easy method for children and amateurs.

Then there were many mechanical contrivances used to take the profile portrait. One was known as the "sheet method." For this an especially made screen was constructed, of which there are many quaint prints.

The one illustrated was found in the second volume of the quarto edition of Lavater's *Essays;* another, used by Chapman in New England is reproduced in Mrs. Carrick's *Shades of Our Ancestors.* Numerous advertisements appeared of "sundry wonderful machines," variants of this mechanical method employed both here and in Europe with most effective results.

Generally a sheet of paper was fastened to the frame work of the silhouette machine, which stood upright between the subject and the artist. It was focused to take the full-size bust picture. The subject seated on a chair at the right of the machine was cast in shadow by candle or lamp-light on to the paper. The artist stood at the left half-hidden by the machine and drew the outline. Says Lavater who used such a contrivance, "Coughing, sneezing, or laughing are to be avoided, as such movements put the shadow out of place."

Usually the silhouette was reduced with perfect accuracy to a smaller size by the pantograph, known as the "Monkey." It was blacked, individualized touches were added, the outline was cut and then it was mounted.

A host of hollow-cutters generally employed mechanical means in drawing a likeness. The profile was made on white paper, and then it was incised with a sharp pen-knife or cut into with scissors, and the hollowed outline was generally mounted on a black ground of silk, velvet, or paper.

This type of silhouette was very common here. Some artists left their portraits unadorned, while others created artistic effects with soft pencilings on the hollowed outline to indicate the hair. Often clothes accessories were sketched or painted on the background — frills, collars, or buttons.

The white-heads which remained after the profiles were hollowed out, are sought by collectors as they frame very effectively against a dark ground.

III

THE PROFILES OF WILLIAM BACHE TAKEN
BY MECHANICAL MEANS

I HAVE not found profile portraits of Jews by all the silhouettists, chiefly, I assume, because so many profilists throve in
New England — Salem, Worcester, Boston, and other places
where the Jewish population was still inconsiderable. But I
believe my collection represents the important different types.

The scrapbook of William Bache, in the possession of his
great-granddaughter, Mrs. C. R. Converse of Elmira, New York,
contains a duplicate collection of nearly two thousand bust
profiles.

These silhouettes are not all of the hollow-cut or painted
variety with which we commonly associate Bache's work, and
of which many exquisite examples can be seen in the Essex
Institute and the Peabody Museum of Salem. In fact, almost
all of the profiles in the Bache Scrapbook were merely blacked
after the profile was mechanically taken; then, cut and pasted
into his album.

That Bache used mechanical means to take a profile is
revealed in the advertisement of his patent machine, discovered
in a Connecticut newspaper of 1810 by Mrs. Carrick. He also
used the pantograph to reduce his portraits; most of those in
the album are three to four inches in size, with a sprinkling
of miniature busts about one and one-quarter inches.

In a minute handwriting in which Bache resorts to curious
quirks and frills and which was extremely difficult to read, he
identifies in long columns at the back of the album, the first
seven hundred or more portraits. Using a magnifying glass I
copied the entire list.

Interesting names appear from all walks of life. Many are of the *haute monde*. General Washington and his wife head the list, followed by Chancellor Wythe, Thomas Jefferson, Mr. and Mrs. Randolph and Major Duval. Some names are prefixed by Doctor, Judge, or General. At times Bache jots down the occupation beside the name of the sitter. I noted a painter, a dancing master, a printer, and comedians.

As Bache traveled far and wide, many names of French, Creole, and Spanish origin appear. Unhappily page after page remain without identification — many plain-looking people, as well as the beauties of the day, some smartly bedecked in quaint millinery.

In addition the album or scrapbook, holds a scattering of delightfully painted profiles in India ink. Ruffles and stocks are touched in with Chinese white, and the exquisite treatment of curls and tendrils, evince Bache's pleasing artistry. Then, too, there was a number of hollow-cuts, their edges embellished by the artist's hand touches, and one white-head, all without identification. Some of the silhouettes are stamped "Bache's Patent," — one word over the other, in an oval, with three minute roses and leaves in between.

Bache was born December 22, 1771, at Bromsgrove, a small town in Worcestershire, England. At twenty-two he came to Philadelphia, where he established himself as a cutter of profiles. As an itinerant artist he traveled much. His work was known in New England, the South and the West Indies. In 1811 he married Miss Anna Page and settled in Wellsboro, Pennsylvania, where he bought extensive tracts of land and ran the general store. Unfortunately an accident befell him there in which he lost the use of his right hand, frustrating his career as an artist. But by that time he had no longer to make a living from his art. He was now a successful business man, and later derived an additional income from his appointment as postmaster of Wellsboro in 1822.

A local history says, "Mr. Bache was a man of strong common sense, well read and with more than ordinary ability. He had a scientific and inquiring turn of mind, was a great lover of Nature, and had a quick and appreciative sense of the ludicrous."

If Bache had identified his entire collection, I am certain many names of Jewish interest would have appeared. A number of profiles are of Semitic appearance, but physiognomy can be as misleading as the name.

However one could be certain of No. 65 in the album, identified as "Jew Pedlar — Dutch." A handsome head with more in it, perhaps, than in his pack. No doubt a descendant of Jews who had fled the Spanish Inquisition. Perhaps someone can identify him for me. His features and bearing bespeak a man of learning. One can picture him traveling about, pack in hand, mulling over idealistic thoughts which had served and would continue to serve his people for generations — their crutch to lean on.

Then there was a Madame Leyva. I venture to say she was a French Jewess whom Bache met in his travels, or one of the Philadelphia Levy's to whose name he had given a fanciful spelling.

I found other names to suggest a Jewish origin. There was a J. Hart in miniature size; he may be Jacob Hart who was buried in the first Jewish cemetery, located in Chatham Square on the Bowery of New York, or John Hart of Baltimore, who identified himself with the Revolutionists. Then I came upon a very plain-looking Miss Pollock, and an L. Pollock, a child's head. There were also a W. Meares, a Harry Elkins, a James Moss, and two silhouettes of Mrs. Henry, one in a delightful looking Quaker bonnet. Do these belong in the Jewish category of portraits?

I V
HOLLOW-CUT PROFILES

EMPLOYING mechanical assistance, the versatile Charles Willson Peale, 1741-1826, was perhaps the first here to make the hollow-cut silhouette in mass production. In this type of silhouette, as previously noted, the profile generally taken by machine is incised from white paper and then mounted on a dark ground. Peale was well-known in his Philadelphia "Museum" as silhouettist, miniaturist, portrait-painter, and sculptor. His profiles are often seen stamped "Museum," "Peale Museum," and "Peale." At times the stamp includes a surmounted spread eagle.

The hollow-cut profile of Mr. Jacob I. Cohen in soldier's uniform sent to me by his great-great-niece, Mrs. D. Grigsby Long, of University, Virginia, is known, she writes, to have been made by Peale.

It is mounted on black ribbed silk set in an oval frame of ebonized wood with gilt inner rim. A newspaper clipping pasted on the back identifies him. A curly lock sweeps his high forehead, offset by wavy hair. His long nose and chin are well-modeled and the lid of his eye and slightly protruding lips are subtly caught.

Jacob I. Cohen was born January 2, 1744, at Oberdorf, not far from Ansbach, Bavaria. He came to this country in 1773. At first he resided in Lancaster, Pennsylvania, then moved to Charleston, South Carolina, where as a patriot soldier he enlisted in Captain Lushington's Company. He participated in the defense of Charleston, and was a member of the expedition to Beaufort in February, 1779.

It was in Virginia that he formed a successful partnership with Isaiah Isaacs, also a member of Lushington's Company. Their dissolution agreement was found written in Hebrew script. Here Cohen became a prominent citizen, a successful merchant and banker. Frequent references found in the Madison Papers show he rendered important services to the young Republic.

He organized the Beth Shalome Congregation in Richmond shortly after the Revolution. Though many of the organizers were of German origin, the service was that known to the Spanish and Portuguese Jews.

In 1782 he married Elizabeth Whitlock Mordecai, widow of Moses Mordecai. She had been born a Christian in England, but embraced Judaism prior to her marriage to Moses Mordecai by whom she had three sons. The well-known Myers family of Richmond, are among her descendants. When she died in 1804, Cohen moved to Philadelphia. He later married Rachel Jacobs, daughter of Israel Jacobs, and became President of the Mikveh Israel Congregation. He died in Philadelphia October 9, 1823.

Identifying Mrs. Israel I. Cohen, is a mellowed newspaper clipping pasted on the back of the ebonized frame, which encloses her hollow-cut silhouette. She was Judith Solomon of Liverpool, born in 1766. Her profile was also sent by Mrs. Long, a great-granddaughter. It is not known who cut the silhouette, with its long and narrow bust line.

She wears a cap with frill, over a protruding forehead, set high atop her well-poised head, and tied with a neat bow at her neck. Her prominent nose, soft mouth, and firm chin are adroitly featured by the artist.

Mr. Israel I. Cohen met Judith Solomon when traveling in Europe in 1787. They were married in Bristol, England, and went to Mr. Cohen's home in Virginia. Seven children, six sons and a daughter, were born to them. A famous son was Colonel Mendes I. Cohen who started in 1830 on a six-year cruise around the world.

When Mr. Cohen died in 1807, his widow moved to Baltimore, where her sons became influential members of the community. Mrs. Cohen died April 5, 1837, when she was seventy-four years old. She was buried in the family burying ground in Baltimore.

In the Cohen Collection of the Maryland Historical Society there is an unattributed hollow-cut silhouette of the animated Mrs. Elijah Etting, (Shinah Solomon) crowned with awry headgear. She was born in Lancaster, Pennsylvania, in 1744, the eldest daughter of Joseph and Bilah (née Cohen) Solomon. In November, 1759, she married Elijah Etting, who was engaged in extensive trading with the Indians. Upon his death, at York, Pennsylvania, July 3, 1778, Shinah moved with her family to Baltimore where she died November 30, 1822.

They were the parents of Reuben and Solomon Etting who played distinguished parts in the early history of American Jewry. Shinah Solomon "always in spirits, full of frolic and glee, and possessing the talent of singing agreeably" captivated Captain Alexander Graydon who writes of her and the hospitality of the Elijah Ettings in his *Memoirs* dated 1773:

York, I must say, was somewhat obnoxious to the general charge of unsociableness under which Pennsylvania had always labored; or if I wrong her, I was not the kind of guest that was calculated to profit of her hospitality. Perhaps I approached her under unfavorable auspices, those of a young man debauched by evil communications; or perhaps there was want of congeniality between her manners and mine. Be it as it may, there was but a single house in which I found that sort of reception which invited me to repeat my visit; and that was the house of a Jew. In this I could conceive myself at home, being always received with ease, with cheerfulness and cordiality. Those who have known York, at this period I am speaking of, can not fail to recollect the sprightly and engaging Mrs. E. (Mrs. Elijah Etting), the life of all the gaiety that could be mustered in the village; always in spirits, full of frolics and glee, and possessing the talent of singing agreeably, she was an indispensable ingredient in the little parties of pleasure which some-times took place and usually consisted in excursions to the Susquehanna, where the company dined, and when successful in angling, upon fish of their own catching.

It was upon one of these occasions, the summer before I met her, that she attracted the notice of Mr. John Dickinson, the celebrated author of the *Letters from a Farmer*. He had been lavish in her praise in the com-pany of a lady of my acquaintance, who told me of it, and then inferred how much I should be pleased with her when I got to York. I paid little attention to the information, having no conception that I should take any interest in the company of a married woman, considerably older than myself, and a mother of several children. The sequel proved how much I was mistaken, and essential to my satisfaction was female society; the access to a house in which I could domesticate myself, and receive attentions, not the less grateful from apparently being blended with somewhat material. The master of the house, though much less brilliant than the mistress of the house, was always good humored and kind; and as they kept a small store, I repaid as well as I could the hospitality of a frequent dish of tea, by purchasing there what articles I wanted.

An album containing some two thousand silhouettes, cut by Todd, around the year 1800, offers some interesting silhouettes of Jews. They are also of the hollow-cut variety.

This collection came into the hands of the Boston Athenæum through Mr. Charles K. Bolton, the well-known librarian and antiquarian, when it was shown him by a Boston bookseller. I think only four hundred dollars was paid for this extraordinary album. Many of the subjects have been indentified as to resi-dence by Mr. Sussex D. David of Philadelphia (S. D. D.), and by Mr. James B. Ludlow (J. B. L.).

Very little is known about the silhouettist, George (?) Todd, whose name Mrs. Carrick located in an 1810 Baltimore directory. His sitters resided all along the Atlantic coast from Massachusetts to Virginia. Many of them, no doubt, stopped at Todd's studio in Baltimore when passing through. Others must have been profiled as he traveled here and there to ply his trade.

In a section preceded by a single page lightly penciled "Baltimore," I found the youthful portrait of Miss Cohen, dainty and smart in starched neckfrill and becoming mobcap. I suppose she was of the illustrious Cohens of Baltimore.

In petal-sprigged cap is Miss Sarah Hays, also known as Sara Ann. I assume she was the daughter of Samuel and Richea Hays. Richea was the second daughter of Michael Gratz, and a sister of Rebecca Gratz. In 1836 Sara Ann married Captain Alfred Mordecai, the first Hebrew to graduate from the Military Academy at West Point. He attained international distinction in military affairs.

A letter from Rebecca Gratz, dated August 27, 1837, to her sister-in-law, Maria Gist Gratz, a gentile, of whom Rebecca was extremely fond, recalls a meeting with her niece, Sarah, at Saratoga Springs. She writes:

Sarah Hays Mordecai is a devoted mother, and rarely has her little Laura out of her arms, it is a sweet little babe — she is going to take it to Richmond, to receive grandfather's blessing — the family are all called together to see perhaps for the last time the venerable old man — his health has been declining ever since you met him here.

The "old man" was Jacob Mordecai, the father of Captain Alfred Mordecai. A son, Alfred Mordecai, Jr., followed in the footsteps of his father, and had a distinguished military career.

In 1893 when she was eighty-eight years old Sara published

Recollections of My Aunt Rebecca Gratz by One of Her Nieces, an important source in the intimate life of the most famous member of the Gratz family.

Sara Ann writes "nothing could be lovelier than her every day life, which commenced every morning with prayers and thanks to the Creator for support and for protecting her through the night, and ended with renewed thanks for the blessings bestowed during the day, while the record of every day's life was a lesson to everyone around her, fulfilling every duty with patience, kindness, humility and love."

The Hays family grace the album in various instances. There is a Mrs. Susan Hay, and a Mrs. Hays; George Hayes and Robert Hayes, but I cannot be certain of their Jewish origin.

"S. D. D." identifies the portrait of Mrs. "Capt." Moses as from South Carolina. She was evidently the wife of Captain Myer Moses II, — a handsome matron with beautiful regular features, gracious and noble in her bearing. I was pleased to find this likeness because another portrait of her, which was considered Sully's, had been seriously impaired by fire, and gave no idea of the beauty of her features.

Her handsome husband also was painted by Sully. Born in Charleston, South Carolina, February 10, 1779, Moses became a member of the South Carolina Legislature and a Major in the War of 1812. Painted in uniform the portrait is one of extraordinary beauty. A large thoughtful-looking forehead framed by a wealth of gray waving hair crowns a face Sully must have delighted to paint.

Mrs. Moses, née Esther Phillips, was born in Philadelphia, July 19th, 1778, daughter of Jonas Phillips and Rebecca Mendes Machado. She married Mr. Moses November 2, 1803, and after their residence in South Carolina, they moved in 1825 to New York. Her name appears in the list of women of the

Congregation Shearith Israel, 1828-1839. Myer Moses died in New York, March 20, 1833, survived by his wife and five children. Mrs. Moses died in Sumter, South Carolina, March 10, 1845.

Sally Sollomon in the section marked "Baltimore," aristocratic debutante, handsome in ruffled fichu is also in the collection, as well as a stunning *beau brummel,* Sam Solomon. His portrait bears the further identification "The Jew," written boldly across the side of the portrait. He appears in ruffled shirt frill, and his hair — though it does not show up in the illustration — is softly penciled on the original mellowed paper, from which the profile is hollowed out.

In an article by Mr. Leon Hühner, *The Jews in the War of 1812,* the name Sam Solomon, 51st Independent Regiment, appears on the "Muster Roll of Citizen Soldiers at North Point and Fort McHenry, September 12 and 13, 1814."

Other names to suggest a Jewish origin are Mrs. "Cap." Abrahams, Mr. Alexanders, Miss Ann Barnett, C. Gideon, Capt. Hayman, Sullon Isaacks, Fanny Jacobs, and R. Jacobs.

Then there is Louisa Meyers, a Mr. Myer with a prominent nose, and a Harriet Myer; a very plain looking Miss Myers appears, a Mrs. Myers of Germanic-Jewish countenance, and Mrs. Mary Myers.

The names Hart, Meyers, and Phillips, with their various spelling forms and large family trees, have always been a nightmare to me — to say nothing of the Franks family, who appeared in *Portraits of Jews.*

From Philadelphia the names, Caroline Phillips and Mrs. Jno. Phillips are perhaps Jewish, as well as Miss Eliza Schwarts, George Solomon, Frank Wise, and a Mr. Zantzinger.

Among these names, I think some interesting identifications will some day be made.

V

FEVRET DE SAINT-MÉMIN

A MACHINE for taking profiles was also used by Saint-
Mémin who perfected the physionotrace invented by
Chrétien, a Frenchman, in 1786. With this instrument,
Saint-Mémin could draw a profile portrait of the face and bust
with minute accuracy.

Miss Mary Martin, an authority on Saint-Mémin, writes in
a monograph, *The Physionotrace in France and America,* that
the apparatus was cumbersome, being five feet four inches
high, but taking the portrait was not a very tiresome process
for the sitter. When the cross-bar and sight were adjusted, an
exact life-size profile of the subject could be traced in a few
minutes.

The son of a nobleman, Charles Balthazer Julien Fevret de
Saint-Mémin was born in 1770 near Dijon, France. At eighteen
he was serving as a royalist in the French Revolution, and
when his army was disbanded he and his family sought refuge
in Switzerland, then came to New York.

The family were now poor; ancestral estates had been confiscated, and as émigrés they took to teaching and gardening
to eke out an existence.

But Charles Fevret de Saint-Mémin who could draw and
paint lived by his art. With the physionotrace he went to
Annapolis, Baltimore, Charleston, New York, Richmond, and
Washington. He made close to a thousand life-size profile
portraits, a number of silhouette busts, painted profiles in
water colors and some charming nature scenes.

His portraits, drawn with black crayon on pink paper,

faithfully produce not only the profile, but the dressing of the hair, the neckwear and the clothing. These bust portraits, about twenty-three by seventeen and one-half inches, were reduced by the pantograph to two inches in diameter and engraved.

The pantograph in the eighteenth century was called the "Stork's Beak" or "Monkey." It is described as consisting "of two triangles so joined by hinges that they resemble a movable square, which is fixed at one point of the base of the drawing, while a point of the larger triangle follows the outline of the life-size silhouette. A pencil attached to the smaller triangle traces the outline smaller, and with perfect accuracy. By repeating these reductions, silhouettes could be made in brooch and locket size." Something like this contrivance is often used by children to reduce the outline drawings found in their picture-books.

Saint-Mémin was very successful in his work. He sold the original life-size drawing, and the reduced twelve engraved prints, to his sitter for thirty-three dollars.

Even at the time it was a good price to fetch, as Copley charged only fifty dollars for a bust portrait and Stuart's price was one hundred dollars. But today Saint-Mémin's charcoal portraits are worth much more than their original cost. When I was assisting the late Mr. Frank W. Bayley, of the Copley Gallery, he asked as much as five hundred dollars for one drawing. Of course, the importance of the subject has much to do with the price of any portrait, especially if it is an excellent example of the artist's work. Saint-Mémin's sitters, who must have paid him about twenty-five thousand dollars, make their gracious appearance in almost all of our eastern Historical Societies.

Two large collections of the engraved portraits were taken

by Saint-Mémin to France. One collection was brought here by J. B. Robertson, an English print seller, and bought by Elias Dexter of New York, who photographed and published it in 1862. This collection numbering seven hundred and sixty-one prints was then bought by Mr. H. L. Carson of Philadelphia, and was sold at auction for forty-eight hundred dollars in 1899.

The second and larger collection was purchased by Mr. Henry Stevens of London, and is now the property of the Corcoran Gallery in Washington. In this collection there are over eight hundred portraits, five silhouettes, and nine views.

Dr. William J. Campbell of Philadelphia, for some time has been collecting the engraved portraits, of which he now has over eight hundred. The Pierpont Morgan Library, the Boston Art Museum, the Metropolitan Museum, and the Bibliothèque Nationale also treasure interesting collections of the engraved portraits.

They are a charming representation of the social, political, and business world of the day. Very handsome are the men, in frilled shirts, unruly locks, or dressed wigs. Among them are the Barclays, the Baches and Beekmans; Washington, Jefferson, and Madison; and the generals, Alexander Macomb and James Clinton. Gracious looking women, too, adorn the collections, their regal heads resplendent in curls and becoming headdress.

A number of portraits are of Jewish interest. Henry Alexander, who was known to have been a Jewish merchant in Baltimore, was drawn in 1803 by Saint-Mémin. His engraved portrait is found in the Saint-Mémin Collection of the Corcoran Gallery.

Abraham Hart of New York had his portrait made in the year 1796. He married Sarah, the daughter of Aaron Storck, who had come from Holland, to these shores, in 1807. Their son, Abraham, born in Philadelphia, married Rebecca Mears of New York, daughter of Samson Mears and Catherine Cohen Isaacks, descendants of exiles of the Spanish Inquisition. The elder Hart's profile is found in the Dexter Publication.

In the Charles Tyler Saint-Mémin Collection in the Boston Museum of Fine Arts, I found a profile of Judge Moses Levy, engraved by Bouchardy, a successor of Chrétien, of Paris. It is a lovely soft engraving representing Levy with a wealth of curly hair, long Semitic nose and distended nostrils, as in the Peale portrait reproduced in *Portraits of Jews*. As the Saint-Mémin profiles are known to be accurate, the Peale portrait must have been an excellent likeness.

Judge Levy, 1758-1826, was the son of Samson Levy, Sr., and the grandson of Moses Levy who came here in 1695. He was graduated from the University of Pennsylvania, which he entered as a student in 1772, and was admitted to the Bar in 1778.

The late Mrs. Robert Hale Bancroft, of Beverly, a great-granddaughter, said he served in the Battle of Trenton, and that she treasured his commission. He also received an invitation to meet General Lafayette when he returned to this country after the Revolution. Levy distinguished himself as a lawyer and Judge and as a member of the Pennsylvania Legislature. He married June 21, 1791, Mary Pearce of Poplar Neck, Cecil County, Maryland. She was one of the bridesmaids to Peggy Shippen, the second Mrs. Benedict Arnold.

Levy's daughter, Martha, became the wife of Hugh Nelson of Virginia. She was also profiled by Saint-Mémin, and the engraving is in volume six in the Collection of the Pierpont Morgan Library.

A drawing by Saint-Mémin of Samson, Jr., 1761-1831, Judge Levy's brother was owned by Mrs. Bancroft. For some time this portrait has been on loan with the Boston Museum of Fine Arts. Samson, too, was a lawyer. He was admitted to the Bar in 1787, and was a member of the Pennsylvania Academy of Fine Arts. He was known as a "unique and curious compound of wit, shrewdness, and courage."

Samson Levy's handsome wife, Sarah Coates, and his mother, gentiles, were also done by Saint-Mémin. They are reproduced in the Dexter Publication.

The Levys were all socially prominent in Philadelphia, where they were members of the exclusive Dancing Assembly. They intermarried, became converts to Christianity, and are buried in St. Peter's Church Yard, Philadelphia.

Mrs. Bancroft was very proud of her Jewish ancestry, and delighted to dwell upon it. She brought forth her genealogical records, tracing her descent direct from Moses Levy, and his second wife, Grace Mears, a Jewess, whom he married in 1718. She displayed the Coat of Arms attributed to Moses Levy, which she had worked out in needle-point upon a large screen, and the family portraits of his descendants. Photographic copies from portraits of Moses Levy and members of his family, treasured by Jewish descendants, which I presented to Mrs. Bancroft were a revelation to her.

On various occasions I visited her and gloried in her veritable museum of paintings, miniatures, silhouettes, exquisite pieces of silver, and furniture. Many of her prized possessions she presented to the Gore Place Society, at Waltham, or placed them on loan there. During my latest visit I noticed hanging on the walls the Rembrandt Peale portraits of Judge and Mrs. Moses Levy.

A small room in Mrs. Bancroft's home was hung almost exclusively with rare silhouettes, many brushed in gold. Among them were portraits of Dr. Arthur Pue of Baltimore, a great-grandfather, and Rebecca Anne Pue, his daughter, who became the wife of Charles Ridgely Carroll. Then there were profiles of Dr. and Mrs. Michael Pue, and of Thomas Poyton Bancroft, Mrs. Bancroft's father-in-law, and his five-year-old son. Judge and Mrs. Samuel Putnam, niece of Timothy Pickering were also there.

But most cherished of Mrs. Bancroft's heirlooms was the family Bible in Hebrew, which belonged to Moses Levy, her great-great-great-grandfather, with entries begun by him, and containing a letter, wafered in, written by his son, Samson Levy, Sr., the father of the brothers — Judge Levy and Samson, Jr.

Very much impressed by the letter I copied it. Samson Levy, Sr., had intermarried; still he clings and desires his children to hold fast to the sacred symbol of their ancestral faith.

My dear Children — or to which soever of your hands this may fall into.

This Book is an Extraordinary Hebrew Bible with annotations or Commentaries on the text —

It was a favourite Book belonging to My Dear Father and Contained the handwriting of him and my Dear Mother for whom I retain the Greatest Affection not withstanding the long time they have been Dead — the former I knew little of but the latter I well remember — in this Book is by them set down or wrote the names and Birth of all their children, & the Death of Some of them by My Self — I therefore recommend this Book to your Most particular Care as an old family Bible with which I hope you will never part but to your latest posterity — as I regard it for My Parents Sake as well as its being an Extraordinary Book of itself — So I hope you will Show the Same regard and affection to my request that I do to My Parents Memmorary —

I am My Dear Child yr   Affectionate Father
                                                                    Samson Levy

New Castle June 4, 1779

My Father Lived in the City of New York in wch place both him and my Mother Died the former in the year 1728 — and the Latter in the year 1740 —

My fondness for my Parents made me fond of what they Esteemed. I hope my children will have no less affection for me —

Samson Levy

The engraving by Saint-Mémin of Hyman Marks of Rich-mond and Philadelphia taken in 1805 may be seen in the Morgan Collection, and in the American Jewish Historical Society. He married Grace Seixas Judah and their daughter, Abigail, married Joseph Newhouse in 1839. A granddaughter is Mrs. Grace N. Lederer of Philadelphia.

The drawing of Solomon Moses, the husband of Rachel Gratz is dated 1798. It was sent to me by his great-grand-daughter, Mary Porter Scott of Saint Louis, who writes,

The portrait is one of my great-grandfather, Solomon Moses, done in the style of St. Memin. It is a life-size head on pink paper drawn with either pencil or charcoal with touches of white paint. The artist has signed the portrait Volney 1798.

I have never been able to learn who "Volney" is and if you can tell me anything about him, I will be grateful. Did St. Memin ever use that name? It is a very nice portrait and done by someone with ability.

Doubtless this "Volney" is Valdenuit who often assisted Saint-Mémin, and the answer to Miss Scott's inquiry is found on the engraved portrait of Solomon Moses, reduced from the original drawing, in the Saint-Mémin Collection, Morgan Library, which reads "St. Memin and Valdenuit No. 27 Pine St. N. York."

Dacosta, who has been included in the list of Jewish subjects by Saint-Mémin, was not a Jew, but a Spanish Catholic, thought the late Mr. Samuel Oppenheim. His full name was Jose Roiz Da Costa. Isaac Dacosta, the Jew, died about 1784, before Saint-Mémin came here. However, the portrait might be that of his son, Samuel.

Saint-Mémin's distinguished pictorial record revealing with

graceful artistry the appearance of our Americans more than one hundred years ago, thus includes a number of members of the Hebrew race. It is not unreasonable to suppose that other names will turn up from time to time. Successful in the pursuit of his work, Saint-Mémin returned to France in 1810, but revisited this country two years later. In 1814 he journeyed back to France where he was made Curator of the Museum of Dijon, a post he retained until his death in 1852.

VI

THE PAINTED TYPE

THE most unusual and in many cases the most beautiful silhouettes with their miniature-like quality belong to the painted type. In this group are a number of profiles which have come to my attention.

Unattributed is the portrait of Aaron Rodrigues Rivera, in the possession of Mrs. Jerome F. Milkman, of New York, who is a descendant of Aaron Lopez, for whom Rivera was named. She writes that the profile is in water color on parchment, the hair and eyes dark brown, and the complexion ruddy. I should think the profile was painted around 1810 when Rivera was a young man.

Aaron was the only son of Abraham Rivera, 1763-1823, and Hannah Lopez, daughter of Aaron Lopez, the merchant prince of Newport, Rhode Island. His grandfather was Jacob Rodrigues Rivera, 1717-1789, well-known in Newport for his spermaceti factories and as an importer. Jacob espoused the Colonial cause, and was forced to flee to Leicester, Massachusetts, but returned to Newport in 1782. He was a public-spirited citizen and observant Jew. His portrait painted by Gilbert Stuart may be seen hanging in the Redwood Library, Newport, a gift from the Rodman family.

The Rivera name had figured prominently for centuries in Seville, Spain. Like the Lopez family, the Riveras lived as Marranos — Jews who outwardly observed Catholicism, but secretly maintained their faith. When Aaron's great-grandfather, Abraham Rodrigues de Rivera came to New York, he and his children had their Catholic names changed in accordance with Jewish rites. The great-grandfather, Abraham, died in Newport in 1765.

The painted profile of Simeon Levy, by an unknown artist, was presented to me by Miss Aline E. Solomons, of Washington, D. C., a great-granddaughter of the subject. In addition Miss Solomons and her sister, Julia, cherish a number of portraits in oil and exquisite miniatures of their ancestors who came here from England, before the Revolution. The sisters impressed me with their devotion to orthodox Judaism — traditional in their family — and interest in all phases of communal activity. Jewishness and Americanism are not incompatible, as we find time and again.

Simeon Levy, born in 1748, was the father of a number of children — Jochebed, Bilhah, Benjamin, Hannah, Miriam, and Julia. The latter married John Solomons in 1818, and died in 1862, at the residence of her son, Hon. Adolphus Simeon Solomons, who was an incorporator and active member of the National Association of the Red Cross, in Washington, D. C. Simeon Levy died December 23, 1825, in New York, and was buried in the cemetery on Eleventh Street, of Congregation Shearith Israel.

He was profiled in water color in 1812, when he was sixty-four years old, seated in a chair, holding an open book of reddish hue. His waistcoat, too, is painted red; his coat is black, and the head and hair, which fall to his neck in softly curled strands, are outlined in pencil. Edged with gold, the portrait is attractively framed in wide gilt and under black painted glass.

Captivating is the unattributed profile of Isaac Aaron Isaacs, son of Aaron Isaacs, born in Boston, October, 1825. It was done when he was about two and one-half years old.

Delightful curls and ruffled neck, skirt and pantalets are painted in black and white on rough cream colored paper. The arms and hands are in natural tints; his shoes are brown and the basket is yellow. The head, however, is hollow-cut mounted over black silk.

The portrait was painted in Boston. This type of silhouette is rare, indeed, as I have seen only one like it, which is owned by Mrs. Maurice Spillane, and that, too, unfortunately remains unattributed.

Isaac Aaron Isaacs married Mary Pyle of Richmond, Virginia, when he was nineteen years of age. By his first wife there were the children, Aaron C., Rebecca, Albert, Henry, and Walter; and by his second wife, Agnes Cohen, there were Clifford and Ernest, who owns the silhouette. Agnes Cohen died at her home in New York, August 23, 1934, aged seventy-seven years. She was a direct lineal descendant of Jewish worthies. Isaacs died March 1, 1897.

His sister-in-law, Miss Gertrude Cohen of New York, who wrote me about the silhouette, writes, "My father's family Seixas originated from Lisbon, Portugal. Both sides served in the Revolutionary War."

I should like to hear from the descendants. Perhaps there are other interesting mementos of this old Jewish family; portraits and miniatures and silhouettes — pictorial evidence of the early Jews who contributed to the industrial and economic wealth of the country, who fought for its defense, and promoted its cultural growth.

The unattributed painted portrait of Mrs. Israel I. Cohen belongs to Mrs. Arnold Burges Johnson of New York, a great-granddaughter. It is certainly very unlike the hollow-cut of the supposedly same person sent to me by Mrs. Johnson's sister, Mrs. D. Grigsby Long. But it is a gracious profile painted in slate-color, enriched with touches of gold; framed in papier-mâché, with acorn and oak-leaf pendant. Writes Mrs. Johnson, "Great-grandmother left to her descendants a rich heritage of indomitable will, courage, and a loyalty to the Jewish faith."

A very finely executed, but unattributed profile is that of Eleazer Lyons. Wearing a black coat and white stock he is pictured against a light-green background. The portrait is in the possession of Mr. John D. Samuel, of Philadelphia, a descendant.

Eleazer Lyons was born in Holland in 1729. His family of Sephardic origin had fled, no doubt, from Spain or Portugal, wrote Mr. Samuel, at the time of the Inquisition. Shortly after Lyons came to this country in 1775, he married Hannah Levy, daughter of Isaac Levy, an Indian trader, of Lancaster, Pennsylvania.

According to tradition in the Lyons family, George Washington breakfasted at the home of the young couple on his march through Lancaster. When he was offered a hot drink, thinking it tea or coffee, he patriotically refused; but on assurance from Hannah Lyons that it was brewed from roasted rye, he drank it down.

Eleazer and his family later moved to Baltimore, then Surinam (Dutch Guiana), and Philadelphia, where he died in 1816. He was buried in the old Spruce Street Jewish Cemetery as was his wife, when she passed away in 1849.

A son, Judah Eleazer, was the father of Reverend Jacques Judah Lyons, Rabbi of the Sephardic Synagogue, Shearith Israel, New York.

Jews who would be cognizant of a past in this country of which they can well be proud, would find it delightful, as well as informing to see the Cohen Collection in the Maryland Historical Society.

It was thrilling, indeed, to visit there and to note the many heirlooms to Jewish Americana contributed, in great measure, by the generosity of Miss Eleanor S. Cohen.

The Maryland Historical Society houses the John Wesley Jarvis portraits of Mr. and Mrs. Solomon Etting; miniatures of Jewish interest by Benjamin Trott and Edward Greene Malbone; precious mementos — jewels, religious ceremonial objects, and interesting shades of my forefathers.

The little known, yet capable artist, Thomas Gimbrède, painted the profile portraits of Solomon Etting, and his second wife, whose maiden name was Rachel Gratz. Lately bequeathed by Miss Cohen to the Maryland Historical Society, they may be seen in the Cohen Room.

Solomon Etting was one of Baltimore's leading citizens, and as he was also profiled by Hubard and Edouart, we shall read more of him later. Mrs. Etting, 1764-1831, was the daughter of Barnard Gratz of Philadelphia, and among her first cousins were the beautiful sisters, Rachel and Rebecca Gratz. In the Cohen Collection is her invitation to attend a Ball in honor of General Lafayette which reads:

BALL TO THE NATION'S GUEST

The honour of Mrs. S. Etting's Company is requested at the ball to be given in welcome of Gen. La Fayette the second night after his arrival.

C. Carroll of Carrollton	I. Meredith
Col. I. E. Howard	I. G. Davies
Gen. S. Smith	R. B. Magruder
Gen. Stricker	James Swan
Col. Bentalon	D. Hoffman
Robert Gilmer	John Thomas

MANAGERS

In the Gimbrède profile, Mrs. Etting is delicately portrayed in a slate-colored bodice, white kerchief and ribboned white mobcap from which tight curls emerge. Solomon Etting's portrait, equally pleasing, is painted in slate-color, relieved by a white and black tinted fichu. Both portraits signed "T.

Gimbrede," are set within gilt ovals and hang from pendants attached to their black ebonized frames.

Gimbrède, a Frenchman, lived for a while in Baltimore among his compatriots, trying various means of earning a living. William Dunlap says he knew him as a miniature painter, an engraver, and teacher of drawing at the Military Academy of West Point, where he stayed until his death in December 1833.

In the Cohen Room there is still another delicately painted water color signed by Gimbrède of Richea Etting, 1792-1881. Within an ornate gilt oval, the portrait is set under black glass with cornered gold spandrels and framed in heavy gilt. The faintly tinted cheeks are shaded in pale green, and her light brown hair is held by a tortoise-shell comb. In her brown-dotted and low-cut bodice, she presents as enchanting a profile as any I have seen.

Richea was the daughter of Solomon and Rachel (née Gratz) Etting, his second wife. There were three other daughters of this marriage; Kitty who married Benjamin I. Cohen, and Shinah and Ellen who with Richea remained un-married.

The late Miss Josephine Etting, Richea's niece, gave the Gimbrède portrait to Mrs. Francis T. Redwood, who pre-sented it to the Maryland Historical Society, March 22, 1927. Mrs. Redwood writes,

I regret I am unable to furnish you with any information in regard to Miss Richea Etting. The only time I ever saw her was when a very little girl, I was taken by my mother to see "Aunt Richea" and "Aunt Shinah."

One of the old ladies, I can't remember which, was in a high, old four-post bed and wore a ruffled cap. The hall-light, a lamp, took my eye particularly at that time as it was just like a picture in my copy of Hans Andersen's Tales.

The Etting and Cohen families have always been intimate with both of father's and mother's families. They lived near each other when my father and Mr. Israel Cohen were boys. More than a hundred years ago — for my father was born in 1819.

With a heart for sentiment, I grieve to think our beauteous Richea, who was clever and witty, as well, grew old without marriage and children. She presented to the Maryland Historical Society a portrait of George Washington, which, as a child, she had seen Gilbert Stuart painting. Like Rebecca Gratz, her mother's cousin, she interested herself in religious education for Jewish children, and was a director in 1857 in the Sunday School Association of the Sephardic Congregation in Baltimore.

This Congregation, comprising Jews of Spanish and Portuguese origin, exerted an influential sway upon the Jewish community, but, unfortunately, it did not last very long, as there were not enough *Sephardim* in Baltimore to maintain it. Frequently they were forced to call on the neighboring German Jews for their *Minyan* — at least ten men — the necessary quorum for public worship.

The Cohens, on whom they would call, were not to be counted on for support. They were *Ashkenazim,* Jews of German origin, who preferred their residence on North Charles Street, for worship, with their own ritual. They had their private cemetery, too, at West Saratoga Street, near Carey; while the Etting Cemetery was located at North and Pennsylvania Avenues. I sometimes wonder, if like the Lowells and Cabots, the Cohens and Ettings, alone, could commune with the Almighty!

Sephardim and *Ashkenazim* now worship together, and social discriminations, as well, have been eradicated. A few Sephardic families have adhered more rigidly than others, perhaps, to their ancestral aloofness. But on the whole they are now crossed by their co-religionists or by intermarriage, so that few families remain untouched by various strains.

On the pretext that one ancestor or a remote ancestor of an ancestor was of Spanish origin, there are some who persist, because it seems to lend social prestige, though without substantial claim, to call themselves Sephardic Jews.

But I leave this subject for enlightenment and interpretation to Dr. Walter M. Kraus, of New York, editor of the *Saint Charles Magazine*, who has done much to make evident the roots of American Jewry. He has been aided in his research by examining old wills, family Bibles, and the marriage certificates of Spanish and Portuguese Jews, which include the genealogies of the contracting parties. Dr. Kraus says that he has also found Jewish ancestry in the genealogies of a surprisingly large number of distinguished Christian American and English families, which is not generally known. Among them are Ludlows, Winders, Rockefellers, Morgans, Fahnestocks, Cabots, and Saltonstalls.

A rich field for inquiry upon the almost untouched subject of assimilation of early American Jewry, is suggested in the letter sent to me some time ago from Mr. Bernard Berenson, of Italy — distinguished art critic, of distant kin:

> I am very grateful for your *Portraits of Jews*. It is interesting, informing, and stimulating. How interesting it would be to have a history of the infiltration of the Jewish element into American life! Of course, only if it were done in an unsectarian spirit, without favour and without sentimentality.
>
> You mention a portrait of Lorenzo Da Ponte. Do you happen to have a photo? I am interested in that pathetic figure.

I remember with pleasure your coming to see us, and I should be pleased to see you again.

1 Tatti, Settignano, remains our address.

Sincerely yours,

B. Berenson

In the Cohen Collection of the Maryland Historical Society is a profile of Mrs. Benjamin I. Cohen painted with fine brush strokes in black and white. "It is a composite profile," writes Miss Eleanor S. Cohen of Baltimore; "A son and daughter sat for the portrait after Mrs. Cohen's death in 1837 which is said to be an excellent likeness." She was Kitty Etting, the fourth daughter of Solomon and Rachel Etting, and sister of Richea to whom she bears a strong resemblance. Her husband, Benjamin I. Cohen, 1797-1845, was the son of Israel I. and Judith Cohen. He was a member of the banking firm, Jacob I. Cohen, Jr., & Brothers, and was one of the seven persons, who on February, 1838, formed the first Baltimore Stock Board. He was a botanist and horticulturist and a talented amateur violinist.

The Cohens lived in a handsome residence at the southwest corner of Charles and Saratoga Streets surrounded with gardens and hothouses. Here they played a prominent part in the social life of Baltimore.

A letter published in the *Maryland Historical Magazine,* December 1919, from James M. Nicholson to his mother, the wife of Judge J. H. Nicholson, chattily describes a Fancy Dress Party which he attended at the Cohen residence. He wrote "many distinguished people were there, among whom were Officers of both the Navy and Army. The presence of the Charming Host and Hostess was felt and acknowledged everywhere . . . there was no effort visible for the events went on as if by Magic, and it was not until the small hours in the

Morning the guests shook hands and said Goodnight — to Mr. and Mrs. Cohen, after this most delightful Evening. The house is rich and expensive, and if anything has been added for this occasion, it was all in keeping with the rest. To tell you who was there, no very hard task, for I might in general terms say — everybody was there who is at all in the habit of attending parties." There were Howards, Halls, and Oldfields, Cohens and Graffs and Madame Patterson-Bonaparte.

VII

WAX PORTRAITS

THE wax portrait modeled in bas-relief was mounted on a board, framed and protected by glass. I have found only one example of interest to my subject of this very charming expression of the profile-portrait.

A wax profile, in color, of Mrs. Nicholas Schuyler — her maiden name was Shinah Simon — was sent to me by Mr. Henry Joseph of Montreal, a descendant of the Gratz family, whose collection of American Jewish worthies is of extraordinary interest.

Shinah was a daughter of Joseph Simon of Lancaster, Pennsylvania, and sister of Miriam Gratz, Rebecca's mother. Dr. Nicholas Schuyler, her husband, was the cousin of General P. S. Schuyler, a friend of George Washington. As a surgeon in the Revolutionary Army, Dr. Schuyler was stationed in Lancaster, where Shinah resided. She died in 1815, at the age of fifty-three in Troy, New York.

In *Rebecca Gratz* by Rollin G. Osterweis, we read that Shinah was not forgiven for marrying out of the faith until the approaching death of her father, Joseph Simon. About to die he sent for several children and intimate friends, to ask what he could do for them. When Rebecca Gratz was called to his bedside she touchingly said, "Forgive Aunt Shinah, grandfather, please." Sending for his daughter the happy reconciliation took place before he closed his eyes.

I think Shinah's wax portrait was done by John Christian Rauschner, who was working in Philadelphia in 1801, at which time, writes Mr. Henry Joseph, the wax portrait was made.

Rauschner was born in Frankfurt, Germany, in 1760, the

youngest son of Christian Benjamin Rauschner, who was a "Modelleur, Stuccateur and Bossirer" in that city. The son plied the same trade in this country working up and down the coast, and paying his way as barber and hairdresser when the art business was slow.

Shinah's profile is very charming indeed. Within a height of four inches she is beautifully modeled. Her eyes are rather bulged; a bandeau encircles a profuse cluster of dark brown curls and earrings. Pearls entwine her neck over which is a thin white scarf, and she holds a watch and chain.

Mrs. Ethel Stanwood Bolton in her unique book *American Wax Portraits* does not mention this charming wax of Shinah Simon, though she does include two others by John Christian Rauschner of Jewish interest, — Mr. and Mrs. Aaron Storck of Holland, who visited this country in 1810 returning the following year. I should like to know who has acquired them since they were last owned by Mr. Charles Henry Hart.

About them Mr. Hart has written that they are "beautifully and delicately modelled and are artistic in their execution. From the animation and expression they could not have been other than excellent likenesses."

We learn from Mrs. Bolton that the modeling of relief groups and portraits in wax was very popular throughout Europe from the middle of the sixteenth century to the close of the eighteenth century. I noted in her work the remarks of Giorgio Vasari, the Italian chronicler, who says that the colors were ground, sifted and mixed with liquid wax. "Nor," writes he, "shall I conceal that modern artists have discovered the method of working in all sorts of colors, so that in taking portraits from life, in half-relief, they make the flesh tints, the hair, and all so life-like that these figures lack nothing but speech."

Eighteenth century America brought out many examples of the profile modeled in wax which can be seen in the collections of the Essex Institute in Salem, the Boston Museum of Fine Arts, the Bloomfield Moore Collection at Fairmount Park, and in various private collections, notably that of Reverend Glenn Tilley Morse.

The modeling of wax portraits is now happily being revived in the work of Miss Ethel Frances Mundy and Miss Ruth Burke.

VIII

WILLIAM JAMES HUBARD

THE scissored type of portraiture, in which the profile is cut free-hand with scissors, from black paper, and pasted on a white ground abounds in my collection.

A silhouette of Solomon Etting by William James Hubard in the Cohen Collection, of the Maryland Historical Society, belongs to this type.

The framed paper-cutter, known as "Master Hubard" was born in Whitechurch in Shropshire, England, in 1809. His grandfather was the German sculptor, Reinhardt, one of whose works, *The Shipwreck*, is in Westminster Abbey.

A gifted youngster, Hubard's free-hand scissor-work in portraiture and landscapes attracted much attention. Like Edouart, he would cut his silhouettes with scissors, merely by a glance at the sitter.

I read about his work in a rare pamphlet entitled, *A Catalogue of the Subjects Contained in the Hubard Gallery; to which is prefixed a Brief Memoir of Master Hubard.* It was printed in New York by D. Fanshaw in 1825, and reposes in the Massachusetts Historical Society.

The youthful prodigy landed in New York in August, 1824, preceding Edouart by fourteen years. Here he established a Gallery at 208 Broadway, open for afternoon and evening work.

The terms of admission were:

50 cents which entitles the visitor to see the Exhibition and obtain a Correct Likeness in Bust cut by Master Hubard, Who, without the least aid from Drawing, Machine, or any kind of outline, but merely by a glance at the Profile, and with a pair of Common Scissors, instantly produces a Striking and Spirited Likeness.

Evidently Hubard did a rushing business in his Gallery, for we read:

Those who wish for Whole Length Figures or their Likenesses Highly Finished in Bronze are advised to call in the Morning; for, as it has become a fashionable Evening Promenade, the Applicants for Likenesses are so numerous that Only the Bust can be taken.

Guided by able management and well advertised in the newspapers, he achieved quite a reputation, for Hubard was not only a good artist, but an *entrepreneur* as well. Wherever he went he became a great success, cutting a likeness in twenty seconds for fifty cents to two dollars. The completed likeness he would often frame in black glass or black frames.

Heralded in Boston, the *Columbian Centinel* of November 16, 1825, spoke of him as "a boy who possesses the peculiar faculty of delineating every object in Nature or Art, simply with a pair of common scissors."

When the self-called "papyrotomist" came here, he set up a studio. Musical compositions were played by a Panharmonicum; the curious were attracted, and they, no doubt, examined his Papyrotomia, or Hubard Gallery of Cuttings. Some were inspired to poetic outbursts in verse dedicated to Hubard on seeing his remarkable collection.

In Boston he was greatly influenced by Gilbert Stuart. When he left for Philadelphia he took up portrait-painting under Thomas Sully, and later painted small full-length portraits in oil. He continued, too, with his silhouette cutting, at which he was so adept, as well as painting profiles in delicate tints, lightly gilded and accented in India ink.

Sympathizing with the South in the Civil War, he invented an explosive for the use of the Confederate Army, and was killed by the bursting of a shell that he was filling on February 25, 1862.

The full-length scissored and bronzed silhouette of Solomon Etting, great-grandfather of Eleanor S. Cohen is a splendid portrait, vibrant with personality. It represents him about ten years younger than the one that was cut by Edouart. Silhouettes with bronze embellishments of this variety, are very rare, as Mrs. Carrick points out, and eagerly sought by collectors.

Solomon Etting was born at York, Pennsylvania, July 28, 1764. He was the son of Elijah Etting who was born in 1724, Frankfort-on-the-Main, Germany. Elijah came to America in 1758 and married Shinah Solomon, daughter of Joseph Solomon, a merchant of Lancaster, Pennsylvania. Her silhouette we have already mentioned.

Solomon Etting married Rachel, daughter of Joseph Simon of Lancaster. His father-in-law, a wealthy trader in the province, was one of the founders of the Pennsylvania Academy of Fine Arts. In Lancaster they entered into partnership under the name of Simon and Etting. Here Solomon played an important role in Masonic affairs. His wife died January 14, 1790, and was buried in the old Jewish cemetery at Lancaster, where her tombstone is still to be found.

Etting then moved to Philadelphia and finally to Baltimore where he married his second wife, Rachel Gratz, the daughter of Barnard Gratz.

During the remaining fifty-five years of his life, Etting devoted himself to many communal activities. He was one of the leading spirits in the movement to influence the Legislature of Maryland to enact the *Jew Bill*.

For this he addressed successive petitions from 1816 to 1826, to make it possible for the Jews to hold public office without first declaring a belief in the Christian religion.

In 1826 when the Bill was passed he was the first Jew to hold public office in the City of Baltimore, where he became a member of the City Council and later served as president of that body.

The information Etting had furnished about the Jews in America, used by Colonel (later Governor) W. G. D. Worthington in an important speech before the House of Delegates, effected the passage of the Bill.

Colonel Worthington was thus enabled to cite the number of heads of Jewish families in Maryland, their wealth, and their contribution to the service of their country. He added "I know an instance, Mr. Etting of Baltimore had a son of talents and acquirements; he spared no pains on him. The youth wished to study Law. The 'Father,' with pain in his heart and tears in his eyes, told him he could not. Even to be an Attorney in a County Court, he would have first to renounce the religion of his father."

When Etting died in 1847, a Masonic historian wrote "he was a man of sterling integrity, of great wit and drollery and was beloved and respected by a large circle of friends and acquaintances. He was distinguished for his considerable and indiscriminate charities and was in his old age affectionately hailed as 'Father Etting.' "

Hubard's most popular silhouettes are the bust portraits which are upward scooped along the bust line in the manner peculiar to his work. Here is one of the celebrated Rebecca Gratz, taken from the original owned by Mr. Jonathan J. Cullen of Philadelphia, mounted on a card the back of which reads, "Cut with scissors by Master Hubard without Drawing or Machine." It also illustrates the book *Rebecca Gratz* by Rollin G. Osterweis.

Rebecca, a daughter of Michael and Miriam (Simon) Gratz was born in Philadelphia in 1781. As a young lady she interested herself in art and literary circles, and was a member of a group of which Washington Irving was one of the leading figures. Through his portrayal of her gracious character to Sir Walter Scott, she became the inspiration for *Ivanhoe*. Rebecca devoted her life to rearing the children of her departed sister, Rachel; to philanthropy and educational pursuits. She was deeply religious and her interest in Hebrew Sunday Schools, and in the Jewish Foster Home, Philadelphia, sprang from a passion for her religion which motivated ennobling deeds. She passed away in Philadelphia in 1869.

The many lovely painted portraits by Sully of Rebecca Gratz and her miniature by Malbone, remain, of course, most appealing of the likenesses of this gracious lady of the Salons.

Exquisite to look upon, she must have enthralled the artists who painted her. Her beauty impressed itself upon Miss Catherine Brittin Barlow, of Washington, who, after reading my article "Portraits of Jews by Thomas Sully", in the *Daughters of the American Revolution Magazine,* February, 1926, wrote me the following:

. . . As a native of Philadelphia, I knew of the Gratz family who were flourishing in my early girlhood and one of the finest memories I have is of having seen Miss Rebecca Gratz — sat near her at a meeting and was so deeply impressed by her personality, that I never forgot it, and your article gave me a genuine thrill.

It was the winter of the Centennial Exposition, 1876, when a great Ball was given. The Committee — under the leadership of Mrs. Gillespie — was composed of women representing the 26 Wards of the City of Philadelphia — each ward having a sub committee with its Chairman. As my father was a public spirited man and in the affairs of the city — my sister and I were appointed to the Committee, of the Ward in which we lived. It was at the final meeting of the entire campaign — that we saw Miss Gratz.

Years have rolled on but that scene has been so fixed in my memory that I could paint it if it were possible. Opposite and near me sat a remarkably beautiful woman, not old, nor young, a little large, and most richly dressed, the exquisite pose of her countenance and repose of her body fascinated me, and I knew very little of what was transpiring around me. She seemed to sit apart a little for she was alone. At that time Jews were not given much friendliness, and I noticed that Mrs. Gillespie gave her a little deference which impressed me as to her importance, and as soon as the meeting adjourned, my inquiry was met with "she is Miss Rebecca Gratz, the sister of Simon Gratz, a family of great means and very philanthropic."

I must add that the copy of Miss Gratz portrait brought her face back to me very vividly, and she bore that same reposeful countenance in later years as in her youth.

IX

AUGUSTIN EDOUART

THE work of the Frenchman, Augustin Edouart, is well-known to admirers of the silhouette. He practised his art chiefly in the British Isles and in America, leaving thousands of portraits signed "Augn. Edouart fecit." They were cut from life, generally full-length, the size eight and one-half inches. He inscribed them with the sitter's name, date and place where taken, and sometimes the home address. Very often they were autographed by the sitter. Edouart cut sil-houettes in duplicate from folded black paper, and, of each, methodically retained a duplicate. Occasionally one runs across a profile cut from white paper and mounted on a black ground.

Augustin Amant Constance Fidèle Edouart — what a galaxy of names — was born in Dunkerque, France, in 1789. He served under Napoleon in his youth and was decorated. But he had a distaste for military life and escaped to England where he married Emilie Laurence Vital. A son, the Rev. Augustus Gaspard Edouart, became Vicar of Leominster.

At first, Edouart earned his living teaching French, and by a curious handicraft — making animal portraits and land-scapes from hair. In the year 1825 he began to cut silhouettes quite by chance when he profiled some friends who were visit-ing him.

From his first patron, Dr. Majendie, the Bishop of Bangor, he received much encouragement. He silhouetted the Bishop's family, too, from which he received orders for forty duplicates.

For thirteen years Edouart traveled far and wide through the British Isles, cutting profiles by the thousand. He charged a few shillings for the profile bust (there were not many); three and six for full-lengths of children and five for adults. His portraits include the nobility, with an especially interesting group of the exiled French monarch, Charles X, at Holyrood Palace in Edinburgh. Also the landed gentry and village folk whose homes he visited or who called at his studio.

In 1839 when Edouart came to the United States he resided at 114 Broadway, New York. As his reputation had preceded him, he became immediately popular, and his studio was thronged. He worked in other important cities, Boston, Brooklyn, Philadelphia, Washington, Baltimore, and New Orleans. During a residence here of ten years, he cut about ten thousand portraits, more life-like than the static photography of a later day.

Individuals from every sphere of life were represented in his albums, among them the American Presidents — John Quincy Adams, Martin Van Buren, William Henry Harrison, John Tyler, Millard Fillmore, and Franklin Pierce. The statesmen, Daniel Webster and Henry Clay were also cut by Edouart, as well as officers in the Army and Navy in resplendent attire.

Some of the most interesting of his profiles were those of family groups with slaves and household pets included, mounted against an interesting interior.

His American sojourn was over in 1849 when he decided to return to England. Sailing from Maryland on the *Oneida,* the vessel was wrecked the nineteenth of December in Vazon Bay off the coast of Guernsey. No lives were lost, and fortunately in the salvaged baggage were fourteen folios with some nine thousand of Edouart's portraits, including a number of the American scene.

In gratitude to the kindness of the Lukis family, with whom

he stayed when taken ashore, Edouart presented the daughter, Frederica, with his valuable albums.

Brokenhearted over the loss of the greater part of his reference collection, he now turned to his native country, settling in Guines, near Calais, where he died in 1861, in his seventy-third year.

The folios came to Mrs. E. Nevill Jackson after she had inserted a notice in the *Connoisseur Magazine,* asking if owners of silhouette collections might allow her to examine them to complete her *History of Silhouettes.* Mrs. Jackson catalogued the Edouart collection, made facsimile photographs, and sold the original American profiles to Mr. Arthur S. Vernay of New York. He classified and exhibited the silhouettes, many of which were later purchased by the Reverend Glenn Tilley Morse.

I read an undated charming appraisal of Edouart's work culled from the *Burlington Magazine.*

How good an artist was Edouart? Was he for instance, a better artist than Raeburn or Lawrence? For my own part we think he was. But in any case he is much more amusing. For he cut out people "as they are" with no nonsense about them. It is evident that many of Edouart's one hundred thousand silhouettes, so vivacious, so witty, so sympathetic, have a genuine artistic value.

Besides those privately owned, Edouart's silhouettes are in the collections of the London National Portrait Gallery, the Victoria and Albert Museum, the Scottish National Gallery, and in the Archivist Museum at Ottawa. In this country many Historical Societies have collected Edouart's work.

A number of profile portraits of American Jews were cut by Augustin Edouart. From the collection of Mrs. E. Nevill Jackson are two portraits of August Belmont. He was born in Alzey, Rhein-Hessen, Germany, December 2nd, 1816, to Simon Belmont and Fredericka Elsass.

Aaron was the original name, but it was the custom to give Jewish children modernized names with a similarity, at least, in the first letter, and the name was changed to August.

The family originated in Germany with Isaac Simon, of Alzey, who took the name Belmont when Napoleon's royal decree in 1808 made it obligatory for the Jews, as well as Gentiles, to adopt family names. It is often thought the original name was Schonberg or Schonenberg, of which Belmont is the literal translation.

But the late Professor Richard Gottheil says such was not the case. His beautiful volume the *Belmont-Belmonte Family* — which makes genealogical reading a delightful pastime — gives Schonberg or Schonenberg a place-name in the "Amt-Alzei" where Jews had lived for centuries, but where no evidence is found of any connection with the Belmont family.

Isaac Simon, he makes clear, was descended from the Belmonte family of either Amsterdam or Hamburg. There were branches residing, too, in England, in the Dutch colonies of South America, and in Jamaica, Asia Minor, and Southern France.

It is not surprising, we read, that the final "e" was dropped from the family name, as French culture had left its imprint with the Napoleonic invasion.

Isaac Simon Belmont died in 1813 leaving four children, of whom the eldest was Aaron Isaac. Aaron's eldest son was Simon, the father of August Belmont. As a landed proprietor, owning vineyards in Alzey and a town house, August Belmont's father was the outstanding Jew of his "amt" or canton, where for many years he was president of the congregation.

At fourteen August Belmont was sweeping the floors without salary, for the Rothschilds, bankers, at Frankfort-on-Main. When his ability for finance was later discovered, he was invested with responsibility, and within three years transferred to the branch house in Naples where he negotiated important matters with the papal government. He spent his leisure visiting art galleries and developed connoisseurship. Years later he became a foremost collector of his generation. For a number of old Dutch and Spanish masters in 1850 he paid some two hundred thousand dollars.

After a residence in Havana, Cuba, where Belmont again represented the Rothschilds, he went to New York, in 1837, and rented a small office at Wall Street. Here he was American representative of his former employers, and founder of the banking house of August Belmont and Company.

In a duel fought at Elkton, Indiana, August, 1841, with William Hayward of South Carolina, Belmont's leg was permanently injured. *The Twentieth Century Biographical Dictionary of Notable Americans,* says that the innocent cause of the duel was Caroline Slidell Perry, whom he married in 1849. She was the daughter of Commodore Mathew C. Perry, who "opened" Japan to Western Nations and niece of Commodore Oliver H. Perry, commander of the American Fleet at the battle of Lake Erie.

The children were Perry, August, Jr., Oliver H. Perry, Raymond, and a daughter, who married Samuel S. Howland. Writing to John Forsyth of Mobile, Alabama, in 1860, Belmont says, "I prefer to leave to my children, instead of the gilded prospects of New York merchant princes, the more enviable title of American citizen, and as long as God spares my life, I shall not falter in my efforts to procure them that heritage."

Belmont's political services were important to the country

of his adoption. In 1848 he was Consul-General in Austria. In 1853 he was appointed by President Pierce Chargé d'Affaires at the Hague, where in the following year he became Minister Resident.

In 1860 he was Chairman of the Democratic National Committee, serving until 1872, when he resigned, but still remained a delegate from New York to every Democratic National Convention and often presiding officer from 1860 to 1884.

He was devoted to the Union and raised and equipped for the Civil War the first German regiment sent from New York City. Lincoln and his advisers were greatly assisted by Belmont during the struggle, when he forcibly impressed the interests of the northern side upon the Rothschilds and influential friends in Europe.

August Belmont died in New York City, November 24, 1890. His services to the nation were his strongest claim to greatness. But he distinguished himself, too, by the charm of his personality, his great wealth which he freely spent, his interest in the turf and his patronage in art circles. To his descendants he left a splendid heritage which they have nobly carried on.

"The Agent of the House of Rothschild," so Edouart inscribed the silhouettes, wears his high-hat with dignity and sports a walking stick in the one portrait. In the other the small featured man, with rumpled hair and bristling moustache, of non-Semitic appearance, stands erect in fashionable attire, hat in hand. The portraits convey more personality than photographs I have seen of him of a later period.

I am invariably asked, if among the early American Jews, there were any professional portrait-painters. Plowing through his Edouart folios, Mr. Morse discovered the profile of Solomon N. Carvalho. Flourishing a palette and brush, he looks like the ubiquitous artist with long hair and tufted chin. It was taken in Washington, March 20, 1841, and autographed by the sitter in graceful gold writing.

Carvalho, born in Charleston, South Carolina, April 27, 1815, attained fame as a painter, an inventor, and writer. Well-known were his portraits of Thomas Hunter and Isaac Leeser. He received a silver medal for his painting, *The Intercession of Moses for Israel*; and his representation of the interior of the Hebrew Synagogue of Charleston, which was founded in 1795, illustrates the book, *The Jews of South Carolina,* by Dr. Barnett A. Elzas.

In 1853 Carvalho accompanied John C. Fremont, as artist and daguerro-typist, on his famous expedition to the West. His published account was called *Last Expedition Across the Rocky Mountains: Including Three Months Residence in Utah and a Perilous Trip Across the Great American Desert to the Pacific*. Vividly described was the journey from Salt Lake City to San Bernardino, and the life of the Mormons and their religion. He was also the author of *The Two Creations,* a treatise on the mosaic cosmogony.

During a residence in Baltimore, Carvalho was a leading member of the Sephardic Congregation, Beth Israel, for which he composed a Hymn at its dedication, September 16, 1857. His wife, Sarah N. Carvalho was interested in the Sunday School modeled from the one created by Rebecca Gratz in Philadelphia. When the Carvalhos moved to New York the Congregation expired.

I should like to hear from Carvalho's descendants, if any, or his collateral relatives. It is interesting to know that he was one of the first Jewish artists on the American scene which now includes many of remarkable talent.

Who was the handsome A. Cohen taken in cut-away in New Orleans, August 6, 1844? Was he as important as his stance bespeaks? Some one will, perhaps, write me about him and other pictorial evidence of the Jewish colony in New Orleans before the Civil War, of which I have very little.

Edouart cuts with befitting dignity the portrait of Dr. Joshua I. Cohen, at Baltimore, December 17, 1840. He was born August 30, 1801, at Richmond, Virginia, the eighth son and ninth child of Israel I. and Judith Cohen. His autographed silhouette is in Mr. Morse's collection.

Graduating as a physician from the University of Maryland in 1823, he became one of the earliest aurists, perhaps, the first in this country. He was also professor of geology and mineralogy in the University of Maryland; a member of the American Philosophical Society, and a founder of the Baltimore Hebrew Hospital. Among his publications was a monograph entitled *Post-Mortem Appearances in a Case of Deafness,* and a catalogue of his collection of autographs and currency of colonial times. His large and valuable library of Hebrew books was catalogued some years ago by Dr. Cyrus Adler and presented by Miss Bertha Cohen and her nieces, Mrs. Arnold Burges Johnson, Mrs. David Grigsby Long, and Mrs. Isaac Cole, Jr., to the Library of Dropsie College, Philadelphia.

Dr. Cohen participated in the struggle which resulted in the removal of Jewish disabilities in Maryland, and when the Jews were granted full citizenship in 1826, he was subsequently elected to membership in the City Council.

The silhouettists had a way of following the socialites to further their business interests. At England's delightful spa, Bath, which was visited by the *beau monde,* they would ply their trade, in the shadow of the famous portraitists, among them, Gainsborough and Reynolds.

Mrs. Jackson's book, *History of Silhouettes,* pictures many of Edouart's profiles taken here. One is of the kindly-looking General Sir Henry Johnson, G. C. B., in picturesque attire with tied wig and knee breeches. His portrait was taken at Bath, February, 1827. His son, Henry Johnson, Esq., profiled at the same time, looks like a dandy, with top-hat and cane.

The old gentleman who entered the King's service in 1761 served for nearly three-quarters of a century. During the Revolutionary struggle, he was stationed in this country, as an officer in the British Army, married the spirited Jewess, Rebecca Franks of Philadelphia, and removed to Bath, where they made their home. Their descendants are of the Peerage.

How I should like to find a silhouette of Rebecca, whose wit and brilliant sallies won much acclaim! She was the daughter of David Franks, the King's agent for Pennsylvania, and the great-granddaughter of Moses Levy who came to New York in 1695.

In this country the black shade was very popular at Saratoga Springs, where Society flocked for the salubrious baths. Rebecca Gratz pictures the life here of the gay forties in a letter to her sister-in-law, Anna Boswell Gratz, dated September 15, 1848.

My dear Ann:

Sara and Mr. Joseph were with us, but a short time, but we enjoyed every moment that was given — they did not arrive at Saratoga early enough to partake of its gaiety — the Fancy Ball of which Mary has sent you an account was over — though had they been there, they would not have attended it being given on Friday evening — the illuminated garden was very beautiful and seemed to realize those memorable descriptions familiar to readers of fairy tales — the Salon must have appeared equally illusive as it was thronged with representatives of every nation, and every period since men and women learned to trick themselves out in fine dresses — our Mary was tastefully arrayed in the rich dress she had last winter when she left me to join the group — we were all bene-fited by our visit to Saratoga — delighted with our journey through New England and grateful to find ourselves at home again.

A fine and sensitive personality is revealed in the portrait of Dr. Jacob De La Motta of Charleston, South Carolina, taken at Saratoga Springs, July 12, 1844, when he was fifty-five years old. It is in Mr. Morse's collection.

The Doctor's father was Emanuel De La Motta, born in the Spanish West Indies in 1761. The family emigrated to Charleston, South Carolina, where Emanuel was brought up amidst the fine cultural Jewish environment for which this city was noted. A well-known citizen, he served in the Revolutionary War and in the War of 1812.

Jacob De La Motta was born in Charleston in 1789. He studied medicine, was a member of the South Carolina Medical Society in 1810, and a surgeon in the United States Army during the War of 1812. He became one of Charleston's leading physicians and took an interest in Jewish communal affairs. A spiritual discourse he delivered at the consecration of the Synagogue Mikveh Israel at Savannah, attracted the attention of Jefferson and Madison, who wrote him an appreciative letter. In 1841 he was appointed by President Harrison Receiver-General for his district.

Arresting attention among the many items of the Cohen Collection of the Maryland Historical Society, are the Edouart portraits of Bernard G. Etting and Solomon Etting, framed in mellowed maple.

Bernard was born in 1806. He was silhouetted in 1840, in frock coat, glove in hand — very elegant, indeed, and mounted against a lithographed background. Collectors find that silhouettes with water-color or lithograph mounts are more rare and expensive than the plain black shade. They are also more captivating. The looped portières draped over Ionic columns, festooned balustrades, and verdurous gardens — even chairs and tables in ample flowing curves, have a grace which bespeaks the age. The settings recall the Victorian interiors in which I like to picture the early and intriguing plays of Jones and Pinero.

Solomon Etting, great-grandfather of Miss Eleanor S. Cohen of Baltimore, is pictured against a sepia water-color background. Standing before a bookcase, holding glasses and top-hat in hand, he gazes through the large over-draped window to the view beyond.

Practically the same background is employed in another silhouette of Etting in the Erskine Hewitt Collection, both cut in 1840. I prefer the latter characterization with its bold penciled lines indicating the rumpled hair, his coat and buttons, and a firm hand in bold relief.

Edouart was the author of *A Treatise on Silhouette Likenesses,* in which he claims "the representation of a shade can only be executed by an outline." He deplores the mechanically taken silhouette, and the painted and gilded type in gaudy array. These he termed *bigarrades* of which the Etting profile would be, perhaps, a mild example.

Solomon Etting, as we know, was one of Baltimore's prominent citizens. Edouart evidently enjoyed his friendship for the former's self-portrait in the Cohen Collection, cut in 1840, was a gift to Etting. It carries the remark by Miss Eleanor S. Cohen, "Autographed and silhouette by himself and given by him to my great-grandfather, Solomon Etting."

In contemplative mood, Edouart pictures himself against a delicately lithographed background. Gracefully he displays his nimble fingers, taking a bit of snuff, perhaps. The blunted finger, which came through injury early in his career, shows up in his silhouette.

The portrait of Reuben Etting, kindly looking and resigned to the infirmity of old age, was cut in 1843, in his eighty-first year. It is from Mrs. Jackson's collection.

Rebecca Gratz in one of her letters writes of him, "We meet as often together as we can, always on the Sabbath at our eldest sister's house. She never goes abroad, but is so hospitable and cheerful that we assemble in pretty large companies there — three generations together — and Reuben looks like a patriarch, at the head of his tribe."

The son of Elijah and Shinah (Solomon) Etting, Reuben was born at York, Pennsylvania, June 6, 1762. A well-known brother was Solomon Etting. As a young man Reuben clerked in a Baltimore bank. A patriot in the Revolutionary War, he threw down his pen to hasten northward when reverberations of War reached Baltimore.

In 1794 he married Frances Gratz, the eldest sister of Rebecca Gratz. Four years later he was commissioned first captain of the "Baltimore Independent Blues" and in 1801 he was appointed United States Marshal for Maryland by Thomas Jefferson.

His sons and grandchildren distinguished themselves in the service of their country. Elijah Gratz Etting became District Attorney of Cecil County, Maryland. Henry was Commodore in the United States Navy. Benjamin became the father of Lieutenant-Colonel Frank Etting, U. S. Army; and Edward was the father of Captain Charles Etting and Lieutenant Theodore Etting, officers in the Civil War.

When Reuben Etting died, June 3, 1848, he was buried in the private cemetery of the Etting family in Philadelphia, leaving children and his devoted wife who passed away four years later.

The silhouette of James Gratz, taken at Philadelphia, August

18, 1843, was found in the Morse Collection. I think he was "Jac" of whom Rebecca Gratz speaks in her *Letters* with tender affection.

He was born in 1788, and graduated from the University of Pennsylvania when only nineteen years of age. James joined the First Troop of Philadelphia City Cavalry. He was a member of the House of Representatives and of the Senate of Pennsylvania; president of the Union Canal Company; and a director of the Philadelphia Institute for the Deaf and Dumb. He remained unmarried and died September 25, 1856.

When the Gratz family suffered from financial reverses, Rebecca wrote to her sister-in-law Maria Gist Gratz, September 10, 1826:

Jac is most depressed of all he has less power to resist the ills of life in whatever shape they may approach him — and he takes the very worst method to acquire fortitude, for he shuts himself off — communes with his own gloomy thought and becomes — if I were to say nervous it would offend him — but at any rate unhappy.

We must not expect always to have the things we wish for in this world but as you say, to make the best of what we have.

James Gratz is pictured with his cane, perhaps, a necessary crutch, for Rebecca writes in the year of his death, to her brother Benjamin, that "Jac's" lameness continues to give him trouble.

The copy from an original Edouart silhouette, framed in bird's-eye maple, of Mrs. Hyam Harris is in the American Jewish Historical Society. Her maiden name was Catherine Nathan and she was born in Amsterdam, Holland, 1781. She married Hyam Harris, probably, in London in 1798, came to Charleston, South Carolina, in 1800, and to New Orleans later, where she died May 6, 1845.

She is depicted full-length and seated, book in hand, holding her spectacles. Well-indicated pencilings outline the neat collar, the puffed elbow-sleeves and becoming cap. The lithographed background with mantel, lamp, settee, and table resembles the one employed for Madame Jumel's profile, taken at Saratoga, which illustrates Mrs. Carrick's *Shades of Our Ancestors*. Edouart's stock in trade were the mounts he kept on hand, as well as letters, a book, or a sheet of paper to be placed in the sitter's hand.

The portrait of a son, Alexander Harris, was taken by Edouart, January 21, 1844. It is in the Morse Collection, but I am not including it here, because of its poor condition. Mrs. Harris's daughter, Isabelle, was also silhouetted by Edouart, as we shall see later.

I saw the late Mr. Erskine Hewitt's album of Edouart's silhouettes when on loan at the Museum of the City of New York. This most absorbing collection was purchased by Mr. Hewitt from E. F. Bonaventure, Inc. They had bought it in Paris. The album is now owned by Mr. Norvin H. Green of New York. Page after page follows of entrancing interest. Many of the silhouettes are enhanced by backgrounds, either lithographed or delicately sketched in sepia water color. Among them is a beautiful portrait of Chin Lung of China. Alexander Macomb, General-in-Chief of the United States Army, and General Winfield Scott are represented. They are stunning in their regimentals; as is Commodore Isaac Hull, who appears before a yellow-tinted lithograph accented in black tones with ships in the distance.

The Erskine Hewitt Collection also contains some interesting Jewish portraits. Jacob Hays, 1772-? is pictured here. He was High Constable of New York City from 1802-1840, and his portrait in oil, painted by J. A. Shegogue hangs in the Governor's Room, City Hall, New York.

Jacob was the eldest son of David and Esther (née Etting) Hays. His father's family emigrated from Holland in the first quarter of the eighteenth century, and settled in New York City and Westchester County where they farmed. There were six brothers whose sons were patriots during the Revolutionary War. Many descendants are now scattered throughout the United States.

The silhouette bears Edouart's flourishing inscription, "High Constable, Sergeant at Arms and Crier of the Court, New York, of Sessions 25 October, 1839." Pictured against a lithographed background of rural simplicity, Hays struts along a gaunt and intent figure masterfully caught by clever fingers.

Illuminating his personality are quaint remarks in an undated newspaper clipping, pasted beside his silhouette in the album which reads:

. . . What Lestocq was to the Parisian, and Townsend to the London, Old Hays is to the New York, nay, to the American Police. He is the Nestor of the police force in this city, and his fame has extended far and wide. . .

Jacob Hays is a "born genius," and early was the peculiar bent of his mind shown. We have found some difficulty in obtaining the most scanty information of his birth, parentage, education, and doings among the evil doers. What we know our readers shall know; as for the rest, we must be content to let that pass. He was born in Westchester County, in this state, in the year 1772, and we are delighted in being able to state positively and upon good foundation that he had a father and mother. Soon after being breeched he was sent to school, and it was while there that he made the first demonstration of what he was "born to" — of that peculiar talent at detecting thieves, and the recovering of stolen property which has made him famous in his own time, and for all time.

In the garden of his parents was a peach tree, his own exclusive property, upon that tree, at the proper season, came some remarkably fine fruit, which was watched in its progress towards maturity with the anxiety of a parent for its offspring. Each individual peach was known and daily apostrophized, and as they grew, so did young Hays' affection grow with and for them. He knew them well, and loved them dearly. How subject is poor humanity to disappointment and vexation of spirit! — in one fatal night that tree was stripped, and when our young hero rose the next morning, he was minus his peaches.

For a moment he abandoned himself to grief — the next he set about finding out the thief. He hastened to his school room, and there to a certain boys desk, which he forced upon, and found, as he had shrewdly suspected, the whole of the stolen fruit, which with the thief whom he seized by the collar, he returned in triumph to his anxious parents. . .

Hays' flair for discovering crime when he became a Constable is further elaborated upon in the forementioned clipping, which quotes from his biography published in the *Unique* by Charles H. Peabody in 1830. It says:

Indeed, it is supposed by many that he is gifted with supernatural attributes, and can see things that are hid from mortal ken . . . or how, can he discover "undivulged crime" — that when a store has been robbed, he, without stop or hesitation, can march directly to the house where the goods are concealed, and say, "these are they" — or when a gentleman's pocket has been picked, that, from a crowd of unsavory miscreants, he can, with unerring judgment, lay his hands upon one and exclaim "you're wanted!" — or how is it that he is gifted with that strange principle of ubiquity that makes him "here, there, and everywhere" at the same moment?

Jacob Hays was married three times. His second wife was Katherine Conroy and his third wife was Maria Post. One of the wives was pictured by Edouart, but which one? She is freely expressed from billowing hem to the angle of her knitting needles, while the bow beneath the chin and cap adds a piquant touch. This silhouette is from Mrs. Jackson's collection.

S. W. Judah is in the Hewitt Album, in very swanky attire with cane, cut in New York, July 25, 1843. It is autographed.

His wife, the daughter of Hayman Levi of New York, was taken in Saratoga in 1844.

I cannot resist the temptation to couple her with Miss J. P. Noah, though their portraits were not taken at the same time or place. Miss Noah's was cut in New York in 1840.

But how much alike these spirited ladies appear in their plaited chignons, narrow waists, hoop-skirts, and rippling hems! So serene and aware of their awareness! What were they talking of one hundred years ago? A war, a peace, their God and children! Are things far different today?

I assume Miss Noah was related to the brilliant Mordecai Noah, Consul at Tunis. He saw beyond the religious note in Jewish life to the equally dominant one — the nationalistic. He pleaded for a Jewish homeland a century ago, wherein his people might live not by toleration, but by right. Where is his silhouette?

Edouart took two handsome portraits of Henry Lazarus in Louisville, Kentucky, May 13, 1844, which are autographed. They are in the Morse Collection. Henry was born in Philadelphia, March 15, 1806, the son of Isaac and Esther (Lyons) Lazarus. His uncle Henry and father were in business in Mobile, Alabama, as early as 1827. Here they had business connections with John Moss, a leading ship-owner of Philadelphia. The Lazarus brothers ended their days in Philadelphia, from whence they had come and Henry died in Paris, October 21, 1868. He and his wife are buried in a mausoleum in Montmatre Cemetery.

Among the numerous beneficiaries of his will dated Paris, November 18, 1867, were the Jewish Foster Home, the Jewish Portuguese Hebra; his nephew, Henry Samuel; and nieces, Madeline d'Alembert and Eleanor Samuel; a kind friend, Mrs. Octavia Raux, formerly proprietress of the Hotel Prince Regent,

Paris; Benjamin George, his dentist, of the Rue Rivoli; and his adopted son and nephew, Henry M. Isaacson, of whom he says: "I feel in him I leave a son (although by adoption only) in whom I confide, and has always proved worthy of our confidence and affection, and, in compliance with our early counsels, is the only member of his mother's children who has married within his own persuasion, which if possible, forms a closer affinity."

Henry Lazarus evidently was obsessed with fear of being buried alive, because, in his Will he makes the unusual request that at the event of his death, his body be kept in a room as long a time as possible, without covering over nose or mouth, that no ice be put about his body, and that his dear wife must be consulted before closing his remains for inter- ment. He also requested that his funeral be conducted simply, free from pomp or show.

Mary Lazarus, née Moss, was the wife of Henry Lazarus. From her expression I like to think she was kind, affable, intelligent. Her silhouette, found in one of the rescued folios in Mr. Morse's possession, is somewhat foxed from immersion. It was also taken in Louisville, in 1844.

Hayman Levy's autographed portrait is in the Morse Col- lection. He was Warden of Camden, South Carolina in 1835; later, Intendant; a prominent merchant and cotton factor; di- rector of the bank of Camden, and its Mayor. Chapman Levy and Hayman Levy fought duels with Camden men.

I learned from the late Mr. Bunford Samuel, of Philadelphia, a descendant, that Hayman Levy's wife was Almeria De Leon, a descendant of Jacob De Leon. One of their boys was killed in the Civil War; another was broken by the hardships en- dured during the war and died shortly afterward. Hayman Levy died in 1865.

Many Jewish names figured prominently in the service of the United States Army and Navy, among them Commodore Uriah P. Levy of the Navy. He was the father of the law for the abolition of the barbarous practise of corporal punishment in the Navy.

Cut by Edouart in Saratoga Springs, August 20, 1842, he is a striking figure, against a lithographed background, in epauleted uniform carrying a halberd, as seen in the Erskine Hewitt Collection. The illustrated duplicate profile is from Mrs. Jackson's collection.

He was born in 1792, the son of Michael and Rachel Levy. His mother of colonial descent, was the daughter of Jonas and Rebecca (Mendes Machado) Phillips. During the War of 1812, Levy was Master of the Brig of War *Argus,* which ran the blockade to France with Mr. Crawford, the American minister to that country, on board. When the *Argus* destroyed twenty-one British merchant-men, the Common Council of New York City, honored the Commodore with the freedom of the city.

Levy greatly admired Thomas Jefferson whose statue by David D'Angers, the French Sculptor, he presented to Congress. Levy also purchased Monticello after Jefferson's death.

When Commodore Levy died on March 22, 1862, he left a large share of his estate for the maintenance, at Monticello, of an agricultural school, for the children of deceased warrant-officers of the United States Navy. The legality of the bequest resulted in considerable discussion, and the property reverted to his heirs from whom Monticello has been repurchased, and at last restored as a national shrine.

Also in the Erskine Hewitt Album was the silhouette of John Moss by Edouart, cut November 5, 1842. The original duplicate silhouette was mounted against a most picturesque lithographed background of docked ships, and an expansive wharf evincing Moss's interests. A copy has recently come into possession of the American Jewish Historical Society.

As Edouart did not resort to caricature, Moss certainly appeared just as he is pictured — a short stocky man, with determined head planted on stooping shoulders — harnessed against the staggering odds of life's vicissitudes. He wears a high hat, frock coat with flapping tails, and carries a cane. It is a very convincing portrait, except for the feet. How could they carry the burden of his worry? But Edouart often did fall down on his feet!

John Moss, son of Joseph Moss, was born in London, England, January 1, 1774. He came to the United States a very poor man in 1793, and married Rebecca Lyons, a Jewess, the daughter of Eleazer and Hannah (Levy) Lyons, of Lancaster, Pennsylvania. They settled in Philadelphia where Moss became a successful merchant, a director in several railroad companies, and a shipping magnate. One of the boats he sailed was the Brig *Tontine,* which was painted in water color by Anton Roux, when it left Marseilles, June, 1825.

Moss was interested in Masonry and in the Jewish community. He was one of the committee here, which marked the first concerted action, since the Fall of Jerusalem on the part of Jews the world over, in behalf of their less fortunate brothers in Damascus.

There the Jews in 1840 were accused of using the blood of a monk for their Passover feast. This horrible and false indictment stirred their communities in Europe and the United States to vindication. Here President Martin Van Buren, through his Secretary of State, John Forsyth, urged the United States Minister at Constantinople to use his influence in behalf of the persecuted Jews.

At this time Rebecca Gratz touchingly wrote to Maria Gist Gratz, August 27, 1840:

What can be done, unless the Governments of Civilized Nations combine to save them — the Jews have no representative powers, and can only act in their individual capacities, the support of the countries of which they are citizens — and the application of their wealth to purchase their brothers lives is all that they can do — and perhaps this is as far as human aid can go. God in his mercy, may touch the hearts of their oppressors, or break the bonds when all visible means fail.

A hundred years have passed. The Jews are still libelled and persecuted in several European countries. But the civilized nations, through the League of Nations, have mandated Palestine to Great Britain as a national homeland for the Jews. By a commercial treaty with England our own Government recognizes and approves the duty of England to facilitate the efforts of the Jews to establish a homeland in Palestine.

Deprived for many centuries of contact with the earth, the Jews have already proved that they are adept with the plow and hammer. No less conspicuous is their achievement in the spiritual and cultural field. The great Hebrew University, many scientific institutions, a prolific literary production, and a Symphony Orchestra testify to the ever throbbing intellectual life of the Jew.

A copy of the silhouette of Mrs. John Moss (Rebecca Lyons), 1777-1864, also reposes in the American Jewish Historical Society, displaying the same lithographed background used with the profile of Mrs. Hyam Harris. White pencilings enhance the value of this graceful example of Edouart's work.

Samuel Lyons Moss, her son, of most refined countenance, his wife Isabelle, their children, and a slave-boy, holding a glass, form an interesting group portrait cut by Edouart, January 15, 1844. It is mounted against a background on which is silhouetted a race-horse, perhaps Mr. Moss's favorite. A copy of the family group is in the American Jewish Historical Society.

Samuel was born in Philadelphia, June 15, 1811. He became a merchant and cotton broker in New Orleans, where he married Isabelle Harris. She was born in Charleston, South Carolina, April 9, 1819, the daughter of Catherine and Hyam Harris. The children represented are Ernest Goodman, 1839-1901 and Ella Amelia, 1843-1911. Ernest, the eldest son, was about four years old when the silhouette was cut, and the daughter, who became Mrs. Barr Du Val was about five months old at the time. Isabelle, the young and attractive mother in slender waist and voluminous skirt, was nearly twenty-five years old when silhouetted.

Edouart loved to portray children, showing them often with their toys and in delightful animated expression. How quaint and charming they appear — the boy in long curls and wearing full-flounced skirt above short trousers of ankle length.

There were seven children in the Moss family. Isabelle took them to Europe, settling there about 1850. Here they were educated. They lived in Düsseldorf, Dresden, and Paris, and took occasional trips to the United States. Isabelle died in Paris, January 8, 1907. Samuel remained in this country traveling extensively. He died in a popular resort for Southerners, the Stevenson House, St. Catherines, Ontario, Canada, August 10, 1870.

In the Erskine Hewitt Collection is the silhouette cut by Edouart, August 21, 1842, at Saratoga Springs, of Henry M. Phillips, "Counsellor at Law," of Philadelphia. He is a short man, pictured with right arm extended as if eloquently pleading a case.

Henry Phillips was born in 1811. His father, Zalegman

Phillips, was one of the leading criminal lawyers of Philadelphia, having graduated from the University of Pennsylvania in 1795. Henry's mother was Arabella, daughter of Myer and Catherine Bush Solomon of Baltimore.

His grandfather, Jonas Phillips, who came to America in 1756, married Rebecca Mendes Machado to whom twenty-one children were born. Among them and their descendants were many who attained distinction. Jonas was a *shocket* (a religious official who slaughters animals according to Jewish ritual), and also took an active interest in civic affairs.

Henry M. Phillips was evidently a man of many interests, as indicated by his varied activities. He was a congressman and a financier, a Master in Masonry, a member of the old Congregation Mikveh Israel, President of the American Philosophical Society, and the Philadelphia Academy of Music. The fountain which stands before the Museum of Art in Fairmount Park, bears the following inscription: "Erected with funds bequeathed for its construction and maintained by Henry M. Phillips who was appointed a member of the Fairmount Park Commission upon its creation in 1867 and served as its President from 1881 until his death in 1884."

His home at 1325 Walnut Street is said to have contained an artistic collection of marbles, bronzes, ivories, and paintings. The latter were willed to Memorial Hall at Fairmount Park when he died, unmarried, in 1884.

Edouart profiled a number of other Jews whose silhouettes I have not obtained. Benjamin Gratz, the brother of Rebecca, was silhouetted at Lexington, Kentucky, where he lived, May 20, 1844. A. K. Josephs was taken at New Orleans, March 20, 1844; his name appears in the first List of Subscribers to the *Occident*. Edward Israel Kursheedt was cut in New Orleans, March 2, 1844; a portrait of Samuel Moss, brother of John

Moss, whose silhouette is incorrectly listed "James Moss, Jun." is owned by Mr. Glenn Tilley Morse.

The *Vernay and Jackson Catalogues* also list a number of names which suggest a Jewish origin, but I have not been able to identify them. They are A. L. Alexander of Georgia, and Isaac Jacob of New Orleans. The names Hart, Hays, and Henry, and Jacobs appear a number of times. There are thirteen named Mayer and two Mayers; one Meyers, and eight Myers, also a number of Philips and Phillips, and the names Simons, Tobias, Vogel, Weil, Wolf, and Wyse confound me. Probably the future will reveal at least some of them as Jews.

X

SOME MISCELLANEOUS SCISSORED PROFILES

A STRANGE little full-length scissored profile of Joseph Andrade, may be seen in the American Jewish Historical Society. It is dated May, 1865, and bears the embossed stamp "G. B. Wood, Jr." I think the latter may have been the artist, George B. Wood, who was born in Philadelphia in 1832.

Andrade was born in Bayonne, France, July 17, 1788. His father, the Grand Rabbi at Bordeaux, was much respected for his extraordianry knowledge of Hebrew, and was an intimate friend of Archbishop Dubois de Sanzay of Bordeaux and Monsieur de Cheverus, once Bishop of Boston.

An American merchant, Mr. Lewis Chastant, became acquainted with Joseph Andrade in Bordeaux, and under his patronage, the latter came to the United States in 1816, settling in Philadelphia at 30½ Walnut Street. Mr. Chastant, perceiving Andrade's business acumen, introduced him to Mr. Stephen Girard, for whom he became financial agent and adviser to other capitalists and leading merchants.

A wealthy Philadelphian left him a legacy of fifty thousand dollars, in real estate, which Andrade rejected, disinterestedly allowing it to go to the heirs. Though he lived as a pauper, he contributed liberally to charitable purposes, and when he died without leaving a will, his property reverted to the children of his brother, Auguste, and his sister Made Oxeida.

An interesting newspaper item dated June 20, 1868, affixed to his silhouette reads that:

The deceased was well-known on "Change," and in fact, by everybody who had occasion to do business on Third Street. His quip-like figure might be seen every day, wending its way along Third and Walnut Streets in the transaction of business. The eccentricity of his dress attracted the attention of all strangers . . .

I know of a scattering of scissored unattributed silhouettes of Jewish interest. Mrs. John Hill Morgan of Brooklyn owns a silhouette of her ancestor, Dr. Henry Meyers, whose family were Christianized. A scissored bust of Daniel L. M. Peixotto, born in Amsterdam in 1800, is in the American Jewish Historical Society. He was a prominent New York physician. A bust portrait of Henry Joseph of Berthier, Canada, is reproduced in the pamphlet, *History of the Corporation of Spanish and Portuguese Jews 'Shearith Israel' of Montreal, Canada.*

The scissored silhouette of Isaac Harby appears in the book *Isaac Harby* by L. C. Moise. The original is owned by Mr. M. E. Harby of Huntington, Long Island. It is unattributed and mounted against a background of scroll-work in black and white.

The genealogy of the Harby family as reconstructed by Isaac Harby of New York, a great-grandson of the subject goes back to fifteenth century England. Nicholas Harby, a Christian, of the County of Cambridge, was the first member of whom there is a record. His son was William, father of Thomas. The latter's son was Clement, whose son Clement, Jr., was knighted at Whitehall in 1669. Some time later he was Consul in Morea where he married a Jewess.

Clement, Jr., and his wife moved to Morocco, where he became secretary to the king and filled the post of Royal Lapidary. Their son, Isaac Harby, as a jeweller, became a very wealthy man. His son, Solomon, was also prosperous, but when the fortunes of the Jews were confiscated with those of the Huguenots, after the Revocation of the Edict of Nantes, Solomon debarked for Jamaica, and in 1781 went to Charleston, South Carolina.

[80]

Solomon married Rebecca, daughter of Myer Moses in 1787. Isaac Harby, born in Charleston, South Carolina, November 9, in the following year, was the first child of this union. He became a school teacher and in 1810 married Rachel, daughter of Samuel Mordecai of Savannah. Later he achieved prominence as a journalist, literary critic, and dramatist. But his greatest claim to fame rests as the spiritual leader of the Jewish reform movement of 1824 in Charleston.

In June, 1828, Isaac Harby left the South for New York with his sister and children upon the death of his wife. Here he resumed his literary work and teaching, but within a brief period, he was taken ill and died December 14, 1828, when he was forty years old.

He is buried beneath an upright stone in the tiny triangular cemetery on the south side of Eleventh Street, in the second burying ground of the Shearith Israel Synagogue. There are not more than thirty graves here, as the cemetery was used only from 1805 to 1829. Some of the burial stones stand erect, some lie flat, for between the *Ashkenazim* and the *Sephardim* there were always distinctions, even in death. The former chose upright stones, the latter lie buried under flat stones to indicate that in death all men are level with the earth.

XI

WILLIAM HENRY BROWN

LAST of the great scissor-men was William Henry Brown. He was born in 1808 in Charleston, South Carolina, of Quaker ancestry. Beginning his career in 1824 with a likeness of Lafayette, he continued cutting silhouettes until 1859-60, when the camera clicked down on the popularity of the shadow picture. He lived until 1882 devoting his latter years to railroad interests.

His silhouettes in which he cut the whole figure very rapidly are often found against lithographed backgrounds. Many of his distinguished contemporaries among whom are John Quincy Adams, John C. Calhoun, Andrew Jackson, and Chief Justice John Marshall, appear in Brown's own work, *Portrait Gallery of Distinguished Citizens with Biographic Sketches*. The litho-graphed backgrounds which were done by E. B. and E. C. Kellogg greatly heighten the interest.

The silhouette of Michael Levy belonging to Mr. Henry S. Hendricks, New York, is mounted in a narrow flattish frame of stained wood such as Mrs. Carrick associates with William Henry Brown.

He is all dressed up in top-hat resting close to the ears and tilted backward. In knee-length coat, breeches, and buckled shoes his costume is complete. Brown indicates his eye, and even the lash very subtly, the long nose, the full lower lip and rounded chin. Brown's old men are significant for their personality.

His wife was Rachel, the daughter of Jonas and Rebecca (Mendes Machado) Phillips, and sister of the well-known lawyer, Zalegman Phillips. While in London she is said to have been presented at the British court.

Michael and Rachel were the parents of Rebecca Tobias and two very distinguished sons, Uriah P. Levy, whom we have already mentioned, and Jonas Phillips Levy, commander of the *U. S. S. America,* during the Mexican War. The latter was survived by three sons, Jefferson M., Louis Napoleon, Mitchell, and two daughters.

Michael Levy died when he was one hundred and four years old in 1839, and was buried at Monticello, Virginia.

Mr. Hendricks also has a reproduction of "The First Steam Railway Passenger Train in America" in silhouette by Brown, the original of which is in the Connecticut Historical Society at Hartford, showing old man Jacob Hays, as one of the passengers.

Another silhouette attributed to Brown is that of John Moss in the American Jewish Historical Society presenting him against a lithographed background — Independence Hall. Identical with this silhouette is one which illustrates my book, *Portraits of Jews,* though the backgrounds are different.

*   *   *

No less important than the painted portraits of the early American Jews are these shades of my forefathers. How interesting it would be if all their original portraits could be collected and exhibited, from time to time, in our various art galleries and institutions! These side-lights of history would furnish ample evidence of the Jews who contributed along with other racial groups to build this country. In the teaching of American Jewish history, I believe it would be helpful for students to view such an exhibition, for it would lend charm and interest to the study of their background here.

Jewish children especially could visualize American-Jewish personalities, whose history they might be prompted to interpret in dramatic form. This would lend a refreshing touch to Sunday School work and even to the patriotic celebrations in our Public Schools, where the children descend from various racial strains. Any racial group aware of a full knowledge of its existence calls for a more enlightened citizenship among its members.

To view the original portraits or reproductions of the American-Jewish forefathers contributes educationally in history and in art to Jew and non-Jew. To the Jew, particularly, it lends dignity to the past and inspiration to the future.

BIBLIOGRAPHY

BIBLIOGRAPHY

BAROWAY, AARON. *Solomon Etting, 1764-1847*, Maryland Historical Magazine, Vol. XV, March, 1920.

BAROWAY, AARON. *The Cohens of Maryland*, Maryland Historical Magazine, Vol. XVIII, December, 1923; Vol. XIX, March, 1924.

BOEHN, MAX VON. *Miniatures and Silhouettes*. Dent, London, 1928.

BOLTON, CHARLES K. *Workers with Line and Color in New England*. In manuscript, at the Boston Athenæum.

BOLTON, ETHEL STANWOOD. *Wax Portraits and Silhouettes*. The Massachusetts Society of the Colonial Dames of America, Boston, 1914.

BOLTON, ETHEL STANWOOD. *American Wax Portraits*. Houghton Mifflin Co., Boston, 1929.

BROWN, WILLIAM HENRY. *Portrait Gallery of Distinguished American Citizens, with Biographical Sketches*. E. B. and E. C. Kellogg, Hartford, 1845. G. A. Baker & Co., New York, 1931.

CARRICK, ALICE VAN LEER. *Shades of our Ancestors*. Little, Brown & Co., Boston, 1928.

CARRICK, ALICE VAN LEER. *Shadows of the Past*, Country Life, August, 1920; *Vogue for the Silhouette*, Country Life, December, 1922; *Novelties in Old American Profiles*, Antiques, October, 1928.

COLQUITT, DELORES BOISFEUILLET. *Distinguished Jews in St. Mémin Miniatures*, Daughters of the American Revolution Magazine, Vol. LIX, February, 1925.

Dictionary of American Biography. Scribner's Sons, New York, 1928.

DUNLAP, WILLIAM. *History of the Arts of Design in the United States*. Edited by Bayley and Goodspeed, Boston, 1918.

EARLE, ALICE MORSE. *Two Centuries of Costume in America*. Macmillan Co., New York, 1903.

ELZAS, DR. BARNETT A. *The Jews of South Carolina*. Lippincott Co., Phila., 1905.

FEVRET DE SAINT-MÉMIN, CHARLES B. J. *The St.-Mémin Collection of Portraits*. Photographed by J. Gurney and Son. Elias Dexter, New York, 1862.

GILLINGHAM, HARROLD E. *Notes on Philadelphia Profilists*, Antiques, June, 1930.

GOTTHEIL, R. J. H. *The Belmont-Belmonte Family*. New York, 1917.

HART, CHARLES HENRY. *The Last of the Silhouettists*, The Outlook, October 6, 1900.

HARTOGENSIS, BENJAMIN H., A. B. *The Sephardic Congregation of Baltimore*, Publications of the American Jewish Historical Society, New York, XXIII, 1915.

HUHNER, LEON, A. M., L. L. B. *Jews in the War of 1812*, Publications of the American Jewish Historical Society, New York, XXVI, 1918.

JACKSON, E. NEVILL. *Ancestors in Silhouette*. John Lane Co., London, 1921.

JACKSON, E. NEVILL. *The History of Silhouettes,* The Connoisseur, London, 1911.

JACKSON, E. NEVILL. *Catalogue of 3800 American Silhouette Portraits by August Edouart*. London.

JEWISH ENCYCLOPEDIA.

LAVATER, JOHN CASPAR. *Essays on Physiognomy; calculated to extend the Knowledge and the Love of Mankind*. Translated from the last Paris Edition by the Rev. C. Moore, L. L. D., F. R. S. London, 1797.

LONDON, HANNAH R. *Portraits of Jews by Gilbert Stuart and Other Early American Artists*. W. E. Rudge, New York, 1927.

LORD, JEANETTE MATHER. *Some Light on Hubard*, Antiques, June 6, 1928.

MILLS, WEYMER. *Collection of Profile Portraits,* The Connoisseur, December, 1909.

MOISE, L. C. *Isaac Harby*. Central Conference of American Rabbis, 1931.

MORAIS, HENRY SAMUEL. *The Jews of Philadelphia*. The Levytype Co., Philadelphia, 1894.

MORGAN, JOHN HILL. *The Work of M. Fevret de Saint-Mémin,* reprinted from the Brooklyn Museum Quarterly, January, 1918, Vol. V, No. 1.

MORRISON, HYMAN, M. D. *The Early Jewish Physicians in America*. A Pamphlet, read before the Boston Medical History Club, February 24, 1928.

Occident and American Jewish Advocate. Vol. I-IX. Philadelphia, 1844.

OSTERWEIS, ROLLIN G. *Rebecca Gratz*. G. P. Putnam's Sons, New York, 1935.

PHILIPSON, RABBI DAVID. *The Letters of Rebecca Gratz*. The Jewish Publication Society of America, Philadelphia, 1929.

Publications of the American Jewish Historical Society. New York, Vols. I-XXXIV.

SHERMAN, FREDERIC FAIRCHILD. *James Sanford Ellsworth; A New England Miniature Painter*. New York. Privately Printed. 1926.

SWAN, MABEL M. *Master Hubard, Profilist and Painter,* Antiques, June, 1929.

The Saint Charles, Vol. I, No. 1, New York, January, 1935.

Twentieth Century Biographical Dictionary of Notable Americans. Biographical Society, Boston, 1904.

VERNAY, ARTHUR S. *A Catalogue of American Silhouettes by Augustin Edouart. A Notable Collection of Portraits taken between 1839-49*. New York, 1913.

WEBB, A. HOLLIDAY. *Gallery Notes pertaining to the exhibition by J. Stowitts, on the "Arts of the Theatre in Java."* Museum of Fine Arts, Boston. August, 1935.

WELLESLEY, FRANCIS. *One Hundred Silhouette Portraits selected from the Collection of Francis Wellesley*. Preface by Weymer Mills. University Press, Oxford.

ILLUSTRATIONS

A Sure and convenient Machine for drawing Silhouettes.

From Lavater.

"A Sure and Convenient Machine for Drawing Silhouettes"
From Lavater's *Essays on Physiognomy.* Quarto Edition, Vol. II
Courtesy of Widener Library, Harvard University

"JEW PEDLAR—DUTCH"
By William Bache
Courtesy of Mrs. C. R. Converse,
Elmira, New York

Facsimile Specimen from Name-List of Silhouettes
In William Bache's Scrapbook
Courtesy of Mrs. C. R. Converse, Elmira, New York

[95]

JACOB I. COHEN
Hollow-cut by CHARLES WILLSON PEALE
Courtesy of Mrs. D. Grigsby Long, University, Va.

MRS. ISRAEL I. COHEN
(Judith Solomon)
Hollow-cut by AN UNKNOWN ARTIST
Courtesy of Mrs. D. Grigsby Long, University, Va.

MRS. ELIJAH ETTING
(Shinah Solomon)
Hollow-cut by AN UNKNOWN ARTIST
Courtesy of the Maryland Historical Society

MISS SARAH HAYS
Hollow-cut by GEORGE (?) TODD
Courtesy of the Boston Athenæum

MISS COHEN
Hollow-cut by GEORGE (?) TODD
Courtesy of the Boston Athenæum

MRS. "CAPT." MOSES
MRS. MEYER MOSES II
(Esther Phillips)
Hollow-cut by GEORGE (?) TODD
Courtesy of the Boston Athenæum

SAM SOLOMON
Hollow-cut by GEORGE (?) TODD
Courtesy of the Boston Athenæum

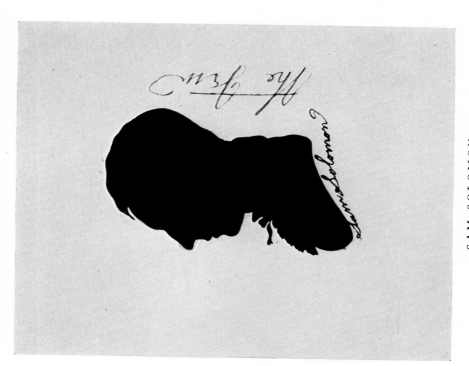

MISS SALLY SOLLOMON
Hollow-cut by GEORGE (?) TODD
Courtesy of the Boston Athenæum

HENRY ALEXANDER
By Fevret de Saint-Mémin
Courtesy of the Corcoran Art Gallery

ABRAHAM HART
By Fevret de Saint-Mémin
From the Elias Dexter
Saint-Mémin Collection of Portraits

HYMAN MARKS
By Fevret de Saint-Mémin
Courtesy of the Pierpont Morgan Library,
New York City

JUDGE MOSES LEVY
By Fevret de Saint-Mémin
Engraved by Bouchardy
Courtesy of the Boston Museum of Fine Arts

SAMSON LEVY, JR.
By FEVRET DE SAINT-MÉMIN
Courtesy of the late Mrs. Robert Hale Bancroft, Beverly, Mass.

SOLOMON MOSES
By FEVRET DE SAINT-MÉMIN
Courtesy of Miss Mary Porter Scott, St. Louis, Mo.

AARON RODRIGUES RIVERA
By AN UNKNOWN ARTIST
Courtesy of Mrs. Jerome F. Milkman, New York City

SIMEON LEVY
By AN UNKNOWN ARTIST
Courtesy of Miss Aline E. Solomons, Washington, D. C.

ISAAC AARON ISAACS
By AN UNKNOWN ARTIST
Courtesy of Miss Gertrude Cohen, New York City

MRS. ISRAEL I. COHEN
(Judith Solomon)
By AN UNKNOWN ARTIST
Courtesy of Mrs. Arnold Burges Johnson, New York City

ELEAZER LYONS
By AN UNKNOWN ARTIST
Courtesy of Mr. John D. Samuel, Philadelphia

SOLOMON ETTING
By THOMAS GIMBRÈDE
Courtesy of the Maryland Historical Society

MRS. SOLOMON ETTING
(Rachel Gratz)
By THOMAS GIMBRÈDE
Courtesy of the Maryland Historical Society

MISS RICHEA G. ETTING
By THOMAS GIMBRÈDE
Courtesy of the Maryland Historical Society

MRS. BENJAMIN I. COHEN
(Kitty Etting)
By AN UNKNOWN ARTIST
Courtesy of the Maryland Historical Society

MRS. NICHOLAS SCHUYLER
(Shinah Simon)
A Wax Portrait
Attributed to JOHN CHRISTIAN RAUSCHNER
Courtesy of Mr. Henry Joseph, Montreal

SOLOMON ETTING
By WILLIAM JAMES HUBARD
Courtesy of the Maryland Historical Society

[135]

REBECCA GRATZ
By WILLIAM JAMES HUBARD
Courtesy of Mr. Rollin G. Osterweis, New Haven, Conn.

AUGUST BELMONT
By Augustin Edouart
Courtesy of Mrs. E. Nevill Jackson,
London, England

AUGUST BELMONT
By Augustin Edouart
Courtesy of Mrs. E. Nevill Jackson,
London, England

[139]

SOLOMON N. CARVALHO
By AUGUSTIN EDOUART
Courtesy of Mr. Glenn Tilley Morse, West Newbury, Mass.

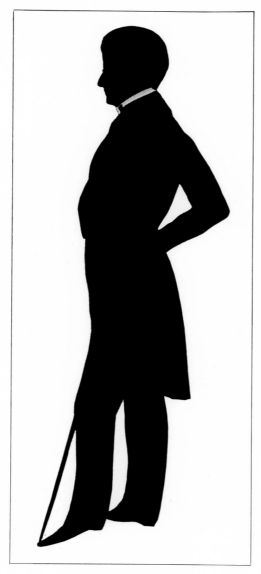

A. COHEN

By AUGUSTIN EDOUART

Courtesy of Mr. Glenn Tilley Morse,
West Newbury, Mass.

DR. JOSHUA I. COHEN
By AUGUSTIN EDOUART
Courtesy of Mr. Glenn Tilley Morse,
West Newbury, Mass.

DR. JACOB DE LA MOTTA
By AUGUSTIN EDOUART
*Courtesy of the late Mr. Erskine Hewitt,
New York City*

BERNARD G. ETTING
By AUGUSTIN EDOUART
Courtesy of the Maryland Historical Society

AUGUSTIN EDOUART
SELF-PORTRAIT
Courtesy of the Maryland Historical Society

[151]

REUBEN ETTING
By AUGUSTIN EDOUART
Courtesy of Mrs. E. Nevill Jackson, London, England

JAMES GRATZ
By AUGUSTIN EDOUART
Courtesy of Mr. Glenn Tilley Morse,
West Newbury, Mass.

MRS. HYAM HARRIS
(Catherine Nathan)
By AUGUSTIN EDOUART
Courtesy of the American Jewish Historical Society

JACOB HAYS
By AUGUSTIN EDOUART
Courtesy of the late Mr. Erskine Hewitt, New York City

MRS. JACOB HAYS
By Augustin Edouart
Courtesy of Mrs. E. Nevill Jackson, London, England

S. W. JUDAH
By Augustin Edouart
Courtesy of Mr. Glenn Tilley Morse,
West Newbury, Mass.

MISS J. P. NOAH   MRS. S. W. JUDAH
                              (née Levi)
          By Augustin Edouart
    Courtesy of Mr. Glenn Tilley Morse, West Newbury, Mass.

HENRY LAZARUS
By AUGUSTIN EDOUART
Courtesy of Mr. Glenn Tilley Morse,
West Newbury, Mass.

[167]

HENRY LAZARUS
By AUGUSTIN EDOUART
Courtesy of Mr. Glenn Tilley Morse, West Newbury, Mass.

Mary Lazarus. late Miss Moss.

MRS. HENRY LAZARUS
(Mary Moss)
By AUGUSTIN EDOUART
Courtesy of Mr. Glenn Tilley Morse, West Newbury, Mass.

HAYMAN LEVY
Mayor of Camden, S. C.
By AUGUSTIN EDOUART
Courtesy of Mr. Glenn Tilley Morse,
West Newbury, Mass.

CAPTAIN URIAH P. LEVY
By AUGUSTIN EDOUART
Courtesy of Mrs. E. Nevill Jackson,
London, England

JOHN MOSS
By AUGUSTIN EDOUART
Courtesy of the American Jewish Historical Society

MRS. JOHN MOSS
(Rebecca Lyons)
By AUGUSTIN EDOUART
Courtesy of the American Jewish Historical Society

MR. AND MRS. SAMUEL LYONS MOSS (Isabelle Harris) WITH THEIR CHILDREN,
ERNEST GOODMAN AND ELLA AMELIA, AND SLAVE BOY
By AUGUSTIN EDOUART
Courtesy of the American Jewish Historical Society

HENRY M. PHILLIPS

By AUGUSTIN EDOUART

Courtesy of the late Mr. Erskine Hewitt, New York City

JOSEPH ANDRADE
By G. B. Wood, Jr.
Courtesy of the American Jewish Historical Society

ISAAC HARBY
By AN UNKNOWN ARTIST
Courtesy of Mr. L. C. Moise, Sumter, S. C.

MICHAEL LEVY
Attributed to WILLIAM HENRY BROWN
Courtesy of Mr. Henry S. Hendricks, New York City

JOHN MOSS
Attributed to WILLIAM HENRY BROWN
Courtesy of the American Jewish Historical Society

INDEX